WE CAME A

5884 (313) Rqıu.C.T, m 2-10-VI. - 4508/A   8593

This document of identity is issued with the approval of His Majesty's Government in the United Kingdom to young persons to be admitted to the United Kingdom for educational purposes under the care of the Inter-Aid Committee for children.

THIS DOCUMENT REQUIRES NO VISA.

PERSONAL PARTICULARS.

Name ULLMANN   FELICIA

Sex FEMALE   Date of Birth 31/12/1936

Place PRAG

Full Names and Address of Parents

ULLMANN   Viktor & Annea

9, Budecska'

PRAG.

BRITISH COMMITTEE FOR CHILDREN
IN PRAGUE.

WE CAME AS CHILDREN

A COLLECTIVE AUTOBIOGRAPHY

edited by

KAREN GERSHON

PAPERMAC

FOR OUR CHILDREN

First published 1966 by Victor Gollancz Limited

First published in paperback 1989 by
PAPERMAC
a division of Macmillan Publishers Limited
4 Little Essex Street London WC2R 3LF
and Basingstoke

Associated companies in Auckland, Delhi, Dublin, Gaborone,
Hamburg, Harare, Hong Kong, Johannesburg, Kuala Lumpur,
Lagos, Manzini, Melbourne, Mexico City, Nairobi, New York,
Singapore and Tokyo

British Library Cataloguing in Publication Data
Gershon, Karen
    We came as children.
    1. Great Britain. Jewish refugees, 1938-1939.
Biographies. Collections
    I. Title
325'. 21'0922

ISBN 0-333-48611-0

Printed in Hong Kong

Dear V.G.,

At the time of the twenty-fifth anniversary of the first children's transports I discovered that most of the documents of those days have been destroyed, and that many of the people who were concerned with our rescue no longer remember the events clearly or, like Anna Essinger, are dead. I decided then to collect what material I could before it was too late.

My request for information appeared in all the major newspapers, putting me in touch with over three hundred people of whom I interviewed about thirty. Two hundred and thirty-four former child refugees have contributed to this book. At first I asked them to write an outline of their refugee lives: later it seemed better to concentrate on the subjects which form the chapters. I thought that everyone who has been through our experiences must have something interesting to say about some of them, and these passages I have selected from each account and discarded the rest.

Nearly ten thousand of us came with the children's transports, most, like myself, through Youth Aliyah. Another thousand were brought by their mothers who came as domestic servants, and others came with both their parents. We all came in transit and there is no record of how many of us eventually stayed. Most of us had a choice at the end of the war; I have confined my enquiry to those who chose England. With their help I have compiled this record, in gratitude and as an explanation.

Yours sincerely,
Karen Gershon.

Ilminster, September 1965.

Twenty or so years ago, somebody said to me that my children were also victims of the Holocaust and I refused to believe it. Time has proved it to be true.

My sister's children, who are Italian, are strangers to mine; they cannot even talk with them. Some of my grandchildren are sabras and they and my English grandchildren are strangers to each other too.

Three of my four children have settled in Israel and at least of the youngest it is true to say that she has done so partly because of the Holocaust – though I never told any of them anything unless they asked me. I chose to marry a non-Jewish Englishman to declare myself (I now see) on the side of life. For the same reason (I believe) she chose an Ethiopian Jew.

When I left my parents I was fifteen years old and I have always believed – or behaved as if I did – that once they reached that age, my children no longer needed me; I am astonished and inadequate when they do. I have more of a relationship with my younger grandchildren than I have with my adult children.

I still cannot have much of a relationship with anyone; I still need to struggle against the feeling that people don't really matter: because my parents were enslaved and killed as if they did not matter and I cannot see anyone, especially myself, as mattering more than they did.

When I came to this country I was on my way to what was then called Palestine. While working on this book I realised that, for me, England would always remain a foster-home. I then continued my journey, together with the family I had made. Perhaps I had left it too late.

I feel more at home in Israel than I do in England, but I don't feel at home there either, and that is worse, because there I still expect to be able to feel at home. Here I am reconciled.

Karen Gershon
St Austell, April 1988

CONTENTS

I am naturally grateful to all the people who have helped me with this book, from those who wrote, from all parts of the world, simply to wish the work well, to those who sent me their unpublished autobiographies. Above all I am grateful to those whose contributions form this book. I gladly acknowledge some of my obligations in detail:

To Mrs. Dorothy Thorneycroft for the letters concerning Paul and to Miss Joan Strange for information about the Worthing Refugee Committee; to Mr. Trevor Chadwick for the account of his work; to Mr. Lawrence Darton for permission to quote from *An Account of the Work of the Friends Committee for Refugees and Aliens* (Society of Friends 1954); to Miss Paula Essinger for an account of her sister's work at Dovercourt and of Bunce Court; to Mrs. V. A. M. Turner for her account of the reception camps; to Mr. Frank Rushbrook for the account of his visits to Dovercourt and his experience as a foster father; to Mrs. Susan Golombok for her account of Dovercourt and to Mr. Robert Kemp for memories of his visit there; to Mrs. A. Mary Howe for her *Soliloquy* and for reports on the work of the Bromley Refugee Committee; to Dr. S. Alexander for the story of the Amsterdam transport; to Werner Pelz for permission to quote from *The Distant Strains of Triumph* (Gollancz 1964); to Mrs. Ruth Wolf for information on foster homes; to John Presland (Gladys Bendit) for the quotation from *A Great Adventure* (Bloomsbury House, July 1944); to Miss L. C. Maynard and Mrs. Lydia Rynes for the accounts of their experiences as foster mothers; to Mrs. Frieda Gilpin and Felicia for permission to reproduce Felicia's landing card and publish her story; to Mrs. Frances Gale for her account of Riversmead; to Mrs. Elisabeth Gordon for the account of her two foster daughters; to Miss Lucie Laquer for her account of Whittingehame House Farm School, to Mr. Arnold Harris for the account of his visit to the evacuees; to Mr. Kenneth Ambrose for the quotation from *The Story of Peter Cronheim* (Constable 1962); to Professor Norman Bentwich for permission to quote from *They Found Refuge* (Cresset Press 1956) and *I Understand the Risks* (Gollancz 1950); and to Mr. C. C. Aronsfeld and the Wiener Library for several sources.   K.G.

1*

EDITORIAL NOTE

I hope that the combination of the different voices will have the same effect as a conversation. Whenever the contributor changes I have marked the beginning of the paragraph thus ¶. Comments from those who were not child refugees are printed in italics.

K.G.

The number of Jewish children who died as a result of the war and the persecution is believed to be about two million. Many died of starvation and hardship and many were killed in pogroms, but there can be no doubt that more than a million were deliberately put to death by the German governmental ordinance.

On arrival [in concentration camps] young children were usually put to death, but . . . boys and girls who were strong enough to work were permitted to live as labourers for a time—usually for six months.

DOROTHY MACARDLE,
Children of Europe, Victor Gollancz Ltd., 1949

ONE CASE

Dear Miss Anny!

My Brother Kurt and Ma wrote me, that I shall bestow on you, about a permit to come to England. I am thirteen years old and I am alone at my parents at home, who are banished, and therefore I must seek a home for me. My parents can't take me along with, and so I pleased you to help me to spend my childhood in England. I should like to come into a Jewish house and I will endeavour me to make you always honour and joy. My dear parents would be very thankfully you would be so kind to help me.

Thank you in advance for your kind help.

Hoping to receive a letter from you I remain yours faithfully,
Paul.

From an undated letter from Anna, a refugee servant, to the Worthing Refugee Committee:

Paul is a German Refugee living since about 3 years in Vienna. His father has been a long time in Dachau concentration camp—is now released and must leave Austria by the end of this month. Parents want to try to get illegal somewhere and Paul must be saved, as his parents cannot take him with them. Paul can't attend school now in Vienna—because he is afraid to go on the street as he was beaten several times already by young Nazi youth. Paul is very intelligent and learns at home from books. His English is quite good. Parents had lost all their fortune at first in Germany and since November they have lost their livelihood in Vienna.

From a letter from the Secretary of the Worthing Refugee Committee to the Secretary of the Movement for the Care of Children from Germany:

June 13th 1939.

I ask you to consider whether you could possibly give a formal guarantee for this child if my committee will promise maintenance and education? We have a promise of two years' hospitality and he could attend the local school; we also have £100 that could be earmarked for him in case the hospitality were not extended.

From a translation of a letter from the boy's father to the Secretary of the Worthing Refugee Committee (Mr. O. Thorneycroft, O.B.E.):

June 30th 1939.

We received a communication from the Kultusgemeinde telling us of your application for our son Paul, and he was put down for a transport which leaves on July 18th. We cannot describe in words the joy of our boy at this knowledge. . . . The expulsion order against me expired on June 28th. . . . We do not know yet where we are to go after the departure of the child.

THE CHILDREN'S TRANSPORTS

I

¶ From my father's diary: . . . a continuous rush and chase from one agency to another; each week new decrees with their requisite documents, etc.; a chaos in which nobody knows what is happening and which, when all is settled, turns out to have been futile.

¶ It was only on the way to the station that our parents informed us that they would have to stay behind 'to clear a few things up'. My brother and I were to travel to England alone. He was seven and I was eight years old.

¶ The prospect of going to England appealed to me above all as an adventure. That we had no relatives or any connection in that country did not deter me. In any case the separation from my parents would be only temporary, since I would be spending at the most two or three years there, just a waiting period until our turn came when we could all be re-united in the U.S.A., our ultimate goal. I was sixteen years old.

¶ I left home with several hundred other children in December 1938. My mother insisted on kissing me over and over again, and I got impatient with her demonstrativeness, not realising of course that this was to be the final parting. I have often wondered since what she must have felt as the result of my impatience. I was eleven years old.

¶ Leaving home—I find I have only vague recollections of seeing my parents at the station, but I seem to remember more vividly the pleasure of the great adventure ahead—going across the sea to England. Somehow I appear to have missed any feeling of wrench, or more probably my parents—who were very sensible—managed not to show any sign of sorrow at the parting. It was all matter of fact, and see you shortly either in London or in Palestine. Rather the kind of farewell that sensible parents give a boy scout off to his first camp. I was thirteen years old.

¶ I remember crying bitterly and saying: 'Please, Mummy, please don't send me away.' I was eleven years old at the time.

¶ My father wrote numerous letters to people abroad in the hope that they could help him to leave, but all in vain. Guarantors, visas, quotas, money—these legal obstacles could not be overcome by him.

¶ I think it is difficult to separate the effects of being a refugee in a strange country from those of being separated from my parents. I was five years old when I arrived.

¶ There was a rumour that Great Britain was prepared to allow several thousand children of Jewish origin to enter the country. It was difficult to obtain reliable information. German newspapers published no such news, foreign newspapers were not always obtainable and foreign news broadcasts were not always reliable or were misunderstood. My mother (my father was in a concentration camp) and I decided that I should travel from my home town to the nearest British Consulate, to find out more about it. This journey was disappointing. Yes, such a scheme was being organised they believed but it had nothing to do with the British Government and they knew no details. They could only suggest that I write to a Committee, the name and address of which they gave me. I returned home a very disappointed young man. It was inconceivable to me that the British Government should have nothing to do with such an undertaking. After all I had grown up in a country where the State controlled everything, and found it difficult to believe that a private committee could do more than distribute charity. But 'committee' like 'visa' became a magic word. Without any intervention or string-pulling I was one of the handful of adolescents who were allotted a place in the first children's transport to leave Germany.

¶ My brother (who was about four years younger than I) came to England before me, because his name somehow got on to an earlier list.

¶ My brother came over to England a few weeks later and was sent to another hostel. I did not see him again for at least three years.

¶ My sister was in her eighth year and I in my ninth—our elder half-sister hoped to come later, but there was no room for her on this transport.

¶ My parents tried hard for us to emigrate. Somehow they

could not manage it fast enough for themselves and decided to send me either to Holland, where we had some very good friends, or to England. The Jewish Hilfsverein in Berlin gave my mother the address of a Mrs. Landmann, who together with her English counterpart, a Mrs. Atkinson, managed to place about a hundred children in England. Mrs. Atkinson owned a farm in Dorset.

¶ An unexpected letter arrived for me from the Vienna Kultusgemeinde asking me to call in two days' time at their offices for registration to England or Holland. Naturally I jumped at this opportunity and after spending many hours there on the specified day, was duly processed and scheduled to go to Holland. This arrangement did not suit me at all and when my father called for me at the Kultusgemeinde bureau I begged him to have my name put down for England. He did manage this after some difficulty.

¶ Some of the children I knew who went to Holland were later returned to Germany and used for medical experiments.

II

¶ *The World Movement for the Care of Children from Germany was the response of the British people to the pogrom of 10th November 1938. The first transport of 320 children arrived at Harwich on 2nd December; when the war broke out 9,354 children had come, of whom 7,482 were Jewish.*

Those who had relations or friends and were therefore individually sponsored were classified as 'guaranteed'. The 'non-guaranteed' were those whose maintenance was undertaken by the organisation itself or by local committees. Jewish children who had no friends or relations in Britain were selected in Germany by the Central Jewish Organisation, the Reichsvertretung, and in Austria by the Kultusgemeinde. The Christian, 'non-Aryan' children were selected in Berlin by the Christian body, Paulusbund, and in Vienna by the Society of Friends.

Lists with particulars and photographs of the children were sent to the Movement in London, and travel arrangements were made on the continent after permits had been issued by the British Home Office and passed by the German police. Priority was given to those whose emigration was specially urgent because their fathers were in concentration camps or at least no longer able to support them, or because they were homeless, or orphaned, or old enough to be in danger themselves. During the first few months several large transports of these children, Jewish and non-Jewish together, reached England. From April 1939, however, individual guarantors had to deposit £50 per head to cover the expenses of future emigration; also, it became difficult to find hospitality for the older boys. The rate at which children could be brought to England therefore decreased.

Trevor Chadwick's Account:

¶ *In 1938 I was teaching at our family prep school. Rumours of the many distressed children in Central Europe reached us, and it was decided to adopt two, according to Home Office regulations, which required a full guarantee of care and maintenance until the age of 18; strict personal references covering the guarantor's character and solvency were also demanded.*

Another master at the school and I set off for Prague to select our pair. We did not know where to begin, and had interviews with various people. . . . Within a few days we had found a couple of small boys of about eight and ten.

We got a clear impression of the enormity of the task. We so often saw halls full of confused refugees and batches of lost children, mostly Jewish, and we saw only the fringe of it all.

Soon after our return I felt that I had to do more about it. I went to Friends House, and later to the Movement for the Care of Children from Germany. They were busy finding guarantors, and I flew back to Prague to find children who would fit in with the guarantors' wishes.

I took my first air transport rather proudly, on a twenty-seater plane. They were all cheerfully sick, enticed by the little paper bags, except a baby of one who slept peacefully in my lap the whole time. The Customs Officers were a little puzzled and began to open some of the suitcases, which contained the kids' worldly treasures. But when I explained the position they were completely co-operative. Then there was the meeting with the guarantors—my baby was cooed over and hustled off, and the other nineteen were shyly summing up their new parents, faces alive with hope for the love they were obviously going to be given. I felt depressed as I returned to Prague. Only twenty! This was late that winter, early in 1939.

But on March 15 the air transports came to an end when the Nazis came in. By then I had a hundred or so children waiting to be sent to England, most of them in odd accommodation in Prague schools, a score in Bratislava, and so on. On March 13 I had a telegram from home—'advise return immediately'—and thinking one of my sons was ill flew back at once. It appeared that war was feared, but it was only the Einmarsch. *I made all haste to fly back, as, while my Prague children were being vaguely fed by Jewish organisations, the Bratislava bunch's rations were rather dubious.*

On the morning of the 15th I got no further than Rotterdam. No flights to Prague. Thwarted and angry I flew to Berlin and began to hammer on tables, except at the British Embassy, where I asked politely for help and was politely refused. Goebbels' office coldly explained that no foreigners could travel to Prague that day (except Germans!). But early the next morning, at the Alexander Platz police station, I was given a special pass enabling me to travel to Prague by train.

A member of the Czech cabinet lent me an office, and I had two young helpers. The whole days, from 7 until 7, with twenty minutes for lunch, were taken up with interviewing, filing and writing letters to the guarantors, which perforce could not be scrappy. I can't say how many children were on my books, but it must have been in the thousands. Nor can I say how many I eventually got away, but it was only hundreds, alas.

Attention had primarily to be paid to the wishes of the guarantors. The majority stipulated girls seven–ten and if possible fair. Boys of twelve and upwards were hard to place. Girls were in the majority on the transports.

I tried to find the most urgent, helpless cases. This was not easy. Many were already refugees from Germany and Austria; many parents had 'disappeared'.

I had contacted a Prague travel agency, because special trains were needed. Now money was getting difficult, and my only hope of financing the thing seemed to be to allow the Movement to pay the travel agency in London, and to ask the connections of the little travellers to pay cash in Prague, or as much as they could afford. Many, of course, were penniless.

The Nazis had arrived. But Kriminalrat Boemmelburg was an elderly, smiling gentleman, far from sinister, who eventually proved to be a great help, sometimes unwittingly. He was really interested in my project, and his only Nazi-ish remark was a polite query why England wanted so many Jewish children.

He happily gave his stamp to the first train transport, even though I had included half a dozen adult 'leaders' on it. I went to the station accompanied by a Gestapo clerk, and all the children were there, with labels prepared by my helpers tied round their necks. The train took them off, cheering, through Germany to the Hook of Holland, a hundred or more.

Soon Boemmelburg sent for me. (He insisted that we spoke in French, not German or English—French is the diplomatic language, he explained. We were both appalling at it.) He said people were throwing dust in my eyes. It was now absolutely forbidden for any adult to leave the country without a special Ausreisebewilligung *and the 'leaders' of my transport had really escaped illegally. I expressed my deepest sorrow and grovelled. I was a blue-eyed boy again, and thereafter he agreed to stamp my lists of children for transport without delay. A kindly Jewess with an American passport was good enough to go with them. I sealed my friendship with Boemmelburg by 'confessing' after the second transport that I had discovered later that one child was not Jewish. (There were several 'Aryans' in all transports.) He praised my honesty and begged me to be careful, because of course the Nazis would look after 'Aryan' children.*

The second train transport was illegal—from the British point of view. Each child on the transport had to be accompanied by a Home Office document, a large stiff affair, foolscap size, perforated across the middle, with a photograph and all sorts of details on each half. These took a long time to arrive. They just didn't realise. If only the Home Secretary could have spent a few days with me, seeing brutality, listening to, not arguing with, young Nazis, as I often did, he would doubtlessly have pushed the whole thing along fast. If he had realised that the regulations were for so many children the first nudge along the wretched road to Auschwitz, he would, of course, have immediately imported the lot. But that is too much wisdom after the event.

I could wait no longer. Letters explaining urgency bore no fruit. I had my guarantors lined up and the children waiting. The next transport was taking shape. There had to be documents, so I had some made, as near as possible like the Home Office ones, and away the train went. I informed everybody and awaited the Home Office telegram in reply. I betted myself that it would contain the word 'irregular' and I won. It also contained a threat to send them back, but I figured the mob of legally accepted guarantors would stop that one.

Boemmelburg remained friendly, and things were going as smoothly as possible. But in the evenings there were other fish to fry which did not have anything to do with children. It became obvious to me as summer developed that certain of my movements were at least suspect, and that B. and his boys might turn sour. This would jeopardize the children, so I explained these things to London and they arranged a replacement. I shall always have a feeling of shame that I didn't get more out.

III

¶ In October 1938 Jews with Polish passports were rounded up by the Gestapo and deported to Poland. We were ditched at the frontier and, together with a large number of other people, we were taken to an old deserted army barracks in Zbonszyn, Poland, where we were given temporary accommodation in terrible conditions. From there we were sent to a hostel near Warsaw where we spent some weeks before sailing for England. My brother was thirteen and I was ten years old.

¶ My parents took me to Prague where after three days of concentrated sight-seeing, shopping and packing, and saying good-bye to people I had not known before and have no recollection of now, I was put on a children's transport with lots of other children of all ages to go to England. I was eleven years old.

¶ We left Vienna sometime during the night, for I remember Mama getting us out of bed, having to dress us, as we were too bewildered and fuddled with sleep to do it properly and quickly. One of my sisters was with me, we were lucky to be able to go together. I was eight years old and she was nine.

¶ During the time my father was in the concentration camp, my mother, trying everything to have him released, was advised by the Jewish committee to send my sister and me to England with the first children's transport leaving Berlin. This terrible decision fell on her shoulders alone—but what else could she do, at least it would mean safety for her children. . . . She sent us not knowing what would become of us or if she would ever see us again. My sister was eleven and I was twelve years old.

¶ My mother took me to Berlin; when I left home my father

was lying in bed ill, the concentration camp had damaged his health. He held me close and bade me look after my mother when she got to England in case he did not make it. I was then just ten years old. We got to Berlin to learn that I was too late for the first transport, but would be able to go on the second. There was of course no money for me to go back home, so my mother took me to friends in Berlin, who kindly put me up for a fortnight or so. My mother had to leave me there, and the last I ever saw of her was in the Berlin Street, outside the friends' house, walking backward along the pavement to get a last look at me, until she rounded the corner and we were parted.

¶ We were allowed one suitcase each containing only clothes. I remember my main worry being that I might not be allowed to take my love tokens—a collection of small cloth animals. My mother, with the insight of selfless love, knew that these objects must be packed in the suitcase at all cost, and reassured me. I was twelve years old.

¶ I left home late in the evening with the whole family to see me off. At the station we were ushered into an enormous waiting room which was packed with children and parents weeping, crying and shouting. It occurred to me there for the first time that our grief was no longer a personal one. We all belonged to a group, but not a group that was determined through social, economic or intellectual dividing lines; we were all refugees. We were ordered to take leave of our relatives quickly and go straight to the train, which had sealed windows and once we were all inside it the doors were sealed as well. Shortly before the train was due to leave our relatives appeared again on the platform. From behind the sealed windows I saw my parents again, rigid and unsmiling like two statues, for the last time ever. I was sixteen years old.

¶ I remember the station and everyone was crying and I did not know why. I was seven years old.

¶ My parents followed us through Berlin from station to station, just to get a few last glimpses of our faces. I was fourteen and my brother was seven years old.

¶ All the children from the different towns met at the Hauptbahnhof in Berlin, each with a small suitcase, ten shillings in German money and a label round our necks giving our names. I was put into a compartment with several other children of my own age—I was eleven, my sister into the adjoining one because she was older. I recall vividly our arrival at the German-Dutch frontier, when the Nazis boarded the train for a last inspection, before it crossed into another country. One Nazi per compartment. . . . The one in our compartment pulled down the blind, made us stand in the gangway, pulled down all the suitcases from the racks, opening them and throwing everything on to the floor. He took one or two small items, really of no value, except a sentimental one. He also asked us for our money, taking the equivalent of nine shillings from each child, and so we left the fatherland with a shilling in our pockets. . . . Fear was in all of us, until the moment the whistle blew, the Nazis left and the train passed over the frontier. At this moment we opened the windows, shouting abuse and spitting at them. . . . It was terrible that we children should have learned such hatred. At the first stop in Holland, we were met by some wonderfully kind ladies who stood waiting for us on the platform with big trolleys, filled with hot drinks, chocolate, sandwiches, etc. . . .

¶ The journey was uneventful as long as we were on German soil. The train was an ordinary passenger train and we sat on the wooden seats, slept as best we could, played games and sang. There were only a few adults with us, so we quite enjoyed the journey. As we crossed the German border, everyone of us, young as we were, felt a tremendous sense of relief. In Holland we got a wonderful reception at each station we stopped at; people crowded the platform and literally showered us with food through the carriage windows.

¶ My sister was unwell with ulcers in her mouth and still convalescing after an appendix operation. I was told to look after her, she was eight years old and I was nine. Of the actual journey I do not remember much, except the hard wooden seats and the long time we were travelling. I remember the train being searched (by the Customs or the Nazis, I didn't know but I was afraid). My sister was in the corner seat by the window and she was asleep. Her head was resting on one of our little string bags, with food for our journey, and I would not let those men look in the bag and disturb her. On thinking of it now, I am surprised that these men ignored us and allowed her to sleep on—but perhaps they were fathers of little girls.

¶ Children under seven years old were meant to go to Holland,

Belgium or France. But my brother who was only two was allowed to come to England with me. When we were going from the train to the boat he was far ahead of me leading the long line of children. He looked like a drummer, with his chamber pot strapped on to his back. I was ten years old and had promised my mother to look after him. But as soon as we had said good-bye to our parents we were separated and we have never lived together again at all.

¶ My sister and I travelled together; I was fifteen and she was sixteen years old. We were given pieces of cardboard with numbers on them which we had to wear on bits of string round our necks. Because my name comes before hers alphabetically, my number was lower and I was always called first when our names were read out and this made me realise that people were not concerned with who we were, our rescue was quite impersonal.

¶ I left home two weeks after my sixteenth birthday. Two compartments were reserved for us—a small number of girls and boys, all of whom I knew well. As we had been told to limit our luggage to one piece, we each had one enormous suitcase, so heavy we could hardly lift it. Leave-taking was restrained and brief. My mother kissed me and the train moved out. It was a final good-bye; I was never to see her again. The trip to Cologne was uneventful. The railway officials were not merely courteous, they were even helpful. I cannot remember what we talked about or even what I felt. My only fear was that we might all be turned back at the frontier, but there was really little likelihood of that since the Nazis were only too glad to be rid of us. Cologne station was the point where we joined other transports and the station was full of many hundreds of children from all parts of Germany from toddlers up to the age of seventeen. When we moved on we were all looking out of the windows for the first sign that we were in Holland. At the first Dutch station a large number of people were on the platform and as our train drew in they waved and cheered—they actually cheered. We were momentarily stunned and then returned the cheers and waved frantically. We were not only free, we were welcomed back to humanity by humanity. There followed a distribution of milk, lemonade, fruit, chocolate, sweets and sandwiches. I doubt if any of us were really hungry, most of us were stuffed with whatever our parents had provided. But this first meal on foreign soil, on free soil, I ate with genuine feeling of gratitude and thanks-giving. This touching reception intoxicated us. The milk might as well have been brandy. Up to then we had been subdued children —understandable in view of our recent experiences and the even more recent separation from our parents. But from this point onwards we were a noisy, boisterous bunch of boys and girls; being our age in fact. Whenever in subsequent years I dreamed about Germany there was always a fog. In these dreams when I was questioned I was unable to answer in English when I was trying to deny my German origin.

¶ Then came the journey by boat across the channel at night, and I remember one little boy in our cabin being violently ill. I was eleven years old.

¶ We embarked at the Hook of Holland at night and arrived at Harwich in the morning. The English customs officer asked us if we had brought any jewellery or other valuables, a question which made us quite indignant. I was eleven years old. We managed to exchange our Germany money for English money, and I was amazed when I saw the size of the pennies.

¶ On the boat, my sister and I were allowed to be together, she was eight and I was nine years old. I remember how worried I was because as we filed aboard an elderly woman with white hair piled on her head was standing at the top of the steps and directed each child, one to the left, the next to the right—I was so afraid that we would be parted, but she waved us on together. We could not find a place to wash and I ventured outside our cabin and asked some 'big' girls where to wash and one of them showed me how the basin came out of the wall. We were very much alone. I can't remember any grown-ups coming to see if we were all right (though perhaps someone did come). I felt very anxious and responsible.

¶ I was ten years old and my total possessions were one small rucksack containing one change of clothes, some socks, handker-chiefs, a mouth organ and some medical supplies for my ear. Also I had 1 Mark 50 Pfening in a little satchet hung round my neck. When the ship berthed at Harwich I wandered about it, leaving my rucksack for a while, and it was a bad loss to find it gone when I returned. People searched high and low but it was not found, so now I had nothing at all except an insignificant amount of worth-less Germany money.

¶ Not only had I never been on a large ocean-going ship but I had never even seen the sea. Alas, it was a night-crossing and I saw very little. The ship had been specially chartered for us. The only adults on board were the crew and those in charge of us. While they were busy I explored the ship, top to bottom, bow to stern. I stumbled into the crew's quarters, engine room and all kinds of places I had no business to be. The only place I was denied was the bridge. Everything I saw was new to me, it was fascinating. My cabin had been allocated to someone more in need of comfort and I spent the night in one of the saloons which had been improvised into a dormitory. Not much sleeping was done there that night. There were about forty or fifty boys, all about fifteen or sixteen years old, in that room. We did not know each other yet. We were all a little over-excited and for the next hours we exchanged, in the dark, all the political jokes which we had picked up. They were mostly variations of 'Hitler, Goebbels and Goering. . . .' The jokes, as such, were not memorable, but the occasion was. We did not need to look over our shoulders or lower our voices and the realisation that we could say what we liked with impunity engendered an atmosphere of enormous gaiety.

THE RECEPTION CAMPS

I

¶ My brother and I arrived in England in the first weeks of December 1938. We were seven and eight years old and I remember nothing of that historic moment except that it was dark and cold, the suitcase I had to carry was very heavy, and Harwich was a very difficult word to pronounce. I felt no sense of occasion or relief at having reached the land of freedom. We had been on the move for so many days now—indeed, so many weeks—that I assumed that we were simply expected to travel on for ever more.

¶ On arrival at Harwich we were met by reporters and committee members. One of the reporters had been looking at me (perhaps because I was small and looked a bit pathetic), anyway, after a few minutes he came over to me, said something I did not understand—so I started to cry—and put a coin into my hand (which I later discovered was a 2/6 piece). He called a nurse over, and took my photo, with the nurse holding the label round my neck, reading it. We had lots of pictures taken, on board, on the gangplank. . . .

We were taken by coach to Dovercourt. It was bitterly cold, and we were housed in chalets, using the main hall for meals, playtime and education in English. It took time getting used to the English porridge and kippers! However, this was a comparatively happy time, I was eleven years old and did not understand. . . . We had fun and I remember learning English songs, like *Daisy, Daisy* and *Underneath the Spreading Chestnut Tree.* . . .

¶ We were told that we must always remember that other children might have come out in our stead and that they might have been more worthwhile people than we. Since then I have always been obsessed with the thought that I must justify my survival.

¶ It was bitterly cold. I remember a large central hall, something like a hangar at an aerodrome with loudspeakers broadcasting messages mainly in English. Here the many children wandered about or crowded round the stoves. We slept in small cabins outside the main building. The beds w re awfully cold and there were not enough of them. I shared one with a boy who probably had scarlet fever; I caught it three weeks later. I did not see much of my sister.

¶ When I fell ill my sister, who was a year older, looked after me. I had a bad throat and kept asking her for a hot drink but the weather was so cold and we were such a long way from the main building that even when she ran with it the drink was always luke-warm by the time it reached me. She thought that I had a temperature and told some grown-up about it. We did not know what the word infirmary meant and anyway I would rather have died with my sister beside me than live and be separated from her.

¶ After a few days at Dovercourt some of us were moved to a small wooden hutted camp near Lowestoft. This was a terribly cold and inhospitable place. After some adverse comments in the press, we were moved and spent a couple of nights sleeping on the floor of a ballroom in a big hotel. Over Christmas we were moved into a large girls' public school near Clacton. This had been very kindly put at the disposal of the committee during the school holidays. The girls had left a variety of toys and little presents for us and we had a marvellous time. After Christmas, it was back to Dovercourt Camp for us.

II

¶ *The first reception centre to be opened was Dovercourt Bay Holiday Camp; Anna Essinger who had a school for refugee children in Kent was asked to take charge of it. She took five teachers and five boys and five girls from her school to help her; the children were to act as go-betweens between her and the refugees. Later she did not want to be reminded of the camp, though she did the best she could with it; she always maintained that it was a terrible experience for those who passed through it.*

¶ *Some of the children were housed in a holiday camp at Kessing-land, near Lowestoft. There was a spell of very cold weather just then and the camp facilities were very inadequate. A member of the staff of St. Felix' School, Southwold, visited the camp and was very distressed by the conditions she saw. She appealed to the headmistress, and when the consent of the school governors had been obtained, a party of 200 boys was taken into the school for a fortnight of the Christmas holidays.*

I was a housemistress at the school at that time, and we got ready at very short notice to receive the boys. The girls departed early in the morning, and the boys arrived that evening. We were under the impression that we should have to deal with very little boys who would need bathing and putting to bed, but when the boys arrived they mostly needed shaving! However we managed to adjust ourselves to the situation, and the boys were very happy to be warm and comfortable. We had many offers of help from people in Southwold, and a cheerful programme of concerts and games was organised.

It was intended that the St. Felix party should go to Dovercourt at the end of December, but a case of infectious disease put them all in quarantine, so for a fortnight one lot went to the Shaftesbury Homes Camp at Dovercourt and some to an hotel at Eastbourne. I went with the Dovercourt party and was taken on to the permanent staff as 'Matron'. This was a very vague title as it included teaching English and Arithmetic, interviewing the Press, and trying to nurse sick boys in very overcrowded double-decker beds.

After about a fortnight we all joined the big camp at Dovercourt. By then all the girls had been moved to another camp in Selsey. There were about five hundred boys and about fifty staff, some German and many English. We were paid £1 a week. The boys and staff slept in chalets, which covered a large area of ground, and we all had our meals in the big dining-hall. The conditions were quite good and we set about organising lessons and games.

The boys were thankful to be safe and comfortable and they were very grateful for the kindness they received, but it did not provide the answer to all their problems. They were naturally fearfully worried about their parents' safety.

Marks and Spencer sent a huge supply of surplus shoes and clothing, so a large store was organised where the boys could be fitted out. A broadcast by the BBC called 'Children in Captivity' produced many kind offers and gifts. An Essex butcher said he would provide beef sausages for all once a week and he did! An anonymous friend sent a dozen cases of fruit every week for several months. A Jewish sporting club used to come down every week-end, and arrange demonstrations of fencing and boxing. Nine Jewish barbers gave up their free time and came down on Sundays to do haircutting.

The Chief Rabbi came down to visit the camp, and planted a tree to commemorate the day. A strong wind and a high tide burst in one night at the lower end of the camp and flooded some of the chalets. At

2

Easter, the camp was wanted, and we chartered a workhouse at Claydon, near Ipswich, and moved there at the end of March.

¶ *After hearing a wireless programme about the children at Dovercourt my wife and I discussed the possibility of doing something. We wrote a letter and the secretary replied saying they would be pleased if we would take some of the children out at any time and generally entertain them, for, as she said, to be at the camp all the time became boring, especially to the older ones. Being in the meat business I also asked whether they would like me to bring anything to help out. She thanked me and said that it would be much appreciated but thought it only fair to tell me that they would not be able to use whatever I brought for the children, as they had all to be treated as orthodox. But the staff, who consisted of many of the Christian faith, would be pleased to have it.*

Well, we went to Dovercourt the following Sunday, and met the secretary who introduced us to four most charming boys about 16–17 years old. We took them out into Clacton, and places around Dovercourt. We always made for Clacton first, because there was a nice restaurant open; being out of season there were not many open on Sundays. These boys all spoke fairly good English, but they made us laugh at times by the terms they used.

We continued to travel our sixty miles (each way) to Dovercourt mostly twice a week, and the boys were always happy with our visit. One Sunday however only three boys were at the gate to greet us, looking very sad. The fourth boy had been taken very ill and was in Dovercourt hospital hovering between life and death. On seeing the boy, I suggested to the camp leader, an Englishman, that his parents be informed by phone at once. Things were getting difficult in Germany regarding permission for Jews to get out even for an emergency. But we thought it worth trying. And the following week his father arrived. Permission had been given to one parent only, who had to sign a declaration that he would return within two weeks. The boy made progress and was doing well by the time his father left. After a month or so he left hospital and came with us to Leigh-on-Sea for a few weeks' convalescence.

¶ *There was a group of very orthodox boys of about ten–thirteen years old at Dovercourt who refused to eat anything except bread because the German Rabbi who supervised the kitchen was not kosher enough for them. I had talks with some of them in my office but nothing helped.*

To avoid separation between brothers and sisters once a boy of two years arrived with his older brother. There were enough of these young ones to run a kindergarten.

The Home Office insisted that the number of children in the camps should be kept constant. When pressure came from Germany we had to take drastic measures to 'sell' the children outside the camp to enable us to save some more from Germany.

¶ *One evening two Rabbis came to the camp and talked to the children. They told them, in very emotional style, that however long they lived they must never forget what they had suffered because they were Jews and the children were all left in a dreadful state. In recollection I have found this very interesting because of two attitudes which one may have about every piece of horror and injustice in the world—one is to try to forget, the other is to see that one never forgets.*

III

¶ I remember realising at Dovercourt that we were in a summer holiday camp and that we as refugees, fleeing in the real sense of the word, had to live here, in the cold chalets by the windy sea because there was nowhere else for us to go. It got so cold that my toes were numb and kind ladies organised parties for us to run up and down the steep sloping beach in order to get warm. I got so cold I did not want even to eat, I must have been a little ill as well. Eating was in the main hall seating hundreds of us at long tables. I remember staying in my chalet under unfamiliar blankets most miserable and cold.

¶ I remember sleeping on a mattress on a crowded ballroom floor somewhere en route from Dovercourt to a convalescent home near Walton-on-the-Naze, which housed us for a time. Now that I was in a smaller community, the earnest *davening** of the boys at Jewish prayer and the Sabbath well and truly celebrated and the services I couldn't attend and the covering of my head with my hands at some Jewish prayers at meals—all these things gave me, who had been brought up as a Christian, a feeling, an actuality of unhappy isolation; although I did learn some Yiddish and I vaguely remember some of the older boys taking

* Yiddish for praying.

me in hand a little, telling me things and smacking me when I picked up a rude word and used it. I did not make any friends, with all the moving, reshuffling and strangeness it would have been difficult I suppose, and one felt always alone. I do not remember any bullying at all as one would get at school. Schooling as such we did not get. There were attempts through songs like *Swanee River*, *Tipperary*, etc. and some desultory lessons to inculcate some basic English. We did a lot of circular dancing, with arms linked, to Hebrew melodies which I remember to this day. But of course I did feel rather alone because I knew very little of Jewishness and it is quite horrible for me to remember now that there was actually religious controversy among some of the Christian and Jewish boys. It was quickly interfered with by the adults, one of whom threatened to send the contestants back to Germany if they did not stop. I do not suppose that she realised that this did not seem such a terrible thing at the time to children parted from their parents.

¶ From Harwich we were taken to a holiday camp at Lowestoft. It was a bitterly cold winter and when we got there the plumbers were just beginning to install a radiator system in the dining- and recreation-halls. It was here that I encountered the delicious novelties of tea with milk, kippers and, best of all, bread with a thick layer of margarine poured over it—no sarcasm intended, I really did enjoy these strange new flavours. After a week or so there, just before Christmas, we moved out and a group of seventy or so boys were quartered in a wing of an old People's Home at Walton-on-the-Naze. This was to be a further very temporary halt while suitable foster-homes were sought for us. It did not work out like that: somebody developed scarlet fever and the whole community was placed in quarantine for four months. Eventually there was a fortnight at a Jewish boarding house at Clacton, a few days at Dovercourt Camp and then a move to a more permanent camp at Claydon near Ipswich.

¶ I was somewhat surprised at being given tea with milk. My mother had stopped putting milk in my tea when I was six or seven, and so I assumed that those in charge thought it healthier for us. Only two or three months later did I realise that tea with milk was the national drink and by the time I was able to try tea without milk I didn't like it any more. I had always slept under a billowing feather bed. Blankets were something I associated with

picnics, holidays and Wild West stories. I was up all the first
night trying to keep warm with the blankets slipping down
either side of the bed and repeated attempts at remaking it in the
dark. The camp was situated on flat ground, very dull country, I
thought. In the distance there was what looked like an enormous
cabbage field rising up against the horizon. I walked towards it
and found, to my surprise, that this cabbage field was the sea. I
rushed down the sand cliff and just stood and looked and looked.
Within a day or two of our arrival severe cold weather set in
quite suddenly; it snowed and the temperature settled well below
freezing point. All water pipes froze solidly and we could neither
wash nor use the lavatories. The kitchen was somehow kept going
but the flimsy wooden huts gave no protection; they could not be
heated and during the night the jugs of water in each hut froze too
and did not melt for several days. Even the urine in the pots
froze. We went to bed fully dressed, wearing scarves and gloves.
Trying to keep warm during the day took up most of our ener-
gies. The camp had to be evacuated hurriedly and I went with a
group of about forty boys to a Salvation Army Sailors' Hostel in
Harwich. The three or four weeks there were the happiest period
for some time to come in our unsettled life. Major and Mrs.
Parker, who were in charge, their daughter and the staff there did
their splendid best to make us feel at home and secure. They succeeded and I still look back with pleasure and gratitude to that
period, so regrettably brief. Our rooms were really cells, each
with a bed and a chair, but they provided privacy, they were
clean and warm. Our presence did not interfere with their normal
pastoral work and the Parkers very kindly put at our disposal two
of their own rooms. One of these was our eating room. The
meals were cooked with care and there always seemed to be more
than was needed—no mean achievement to feed about forty adolescents with ferocious appetites. There was no mass feeding, it
was just like taking meals in a very large family. Our own duties
were light, we made our beds, cleaned our rooms and by rota
helped with the washing up. Every afternoon we went for a long
walk along the seafront of Dovercourt Bay which adjoins Harwich. We gradually explored the country around us, but the walk
along the promenade was our favourite. We never tired of watching the sea. In charge of our little group were two adults, both in
their late twenties, both refugees. They taught us those German

songs which the Nazis had discouraged if not banned. These we were to sing while we marched in a column of three through the town and along the front. We were not to be sloppy and make the place look untidy. It was most important that we made a good impression on the townspeople. Within three days the Mayor 'requested' us to stop marching and singing. The townspeople, far from being impressed, strongly disapproved of such a quasi-militaristic display. We were delighted. One cannot 'march' for a walk and I had always disliked community singing in any form. Henceforth we just walked, an untidy straggling group chattering away anyhow. It was the beginning of our assimilation. The Mayor of Harwich paid us an official visit and we got a mention in the local paper. We became regular visitors of Woolworth and the Post Office, and were presented with free tickets to the cinema and the pantomime. The latter was very puzzling. I thought it was a kind of operetta but could not find out the name of the composer. The jokes, such as they were, passed me by. Early in January we were transferred to the Camp at Dovercourt Bay. Inevitably, the atmosphere there was impersonal, a fact which was driven home forcefully when our group, against our wishes and voluble protests, was split up.

There were classes in which English was taught, and numerous lectures. Lectures on current affairs, on Great Britain, on the Empire, and lectures on the customs of the country, on how to behave and how not to behave, i.e. not to talk German loudly in public, better still not to talk loudly at all, how to exercise tact in our—as yet limited—contacts with the English. A great slice of my time was taken up with writing letters to my parents. These letters got longer and longer and were quite a feature of my life at that time. Like any other boy of sixteen I disliked writing letters but after I left home I became an assiduous letter-writer not only to my parents but to my then still numerous relations and later to my friends. On leaving home I was asked to write often and I did; at first from a sense of duty, then because there was so much to write about. I used to boast during my first years here that I never suffered from homesickness. I now realise that this frantic letter-writing was just that. I wrote in detail about important things as well as trivialities, good news and bad news. I learned later that my reports about the freezing up of Pakefield Hall and the partial flooding of the Dovercourt Camp caused my parents bitterly to reproach themselves for having let me go to England. Yet it never occurred to me that my letters would have such an effect because I never for a moment regretted that I had come. Any hardship I countered with the thought: 'Better this than being in Germany.'

IV

¶ Every day enquiries from prospective foster-parents arrived at the camp. One day one of the officials at the camp came up to me in the dining-hall and asked whether I was orthodox. I didn't know whether to say yes or no because I didn't really know how orthodox I was. I looked at my friend sitting opposite me. She nodded her head. I said 'yes' and the next day was sent off to Liverpool to a family who wanted a girl my age as company for their daughter. I realise now that that nod of the head from my friend probably determined the whole course of my future life. I remember feeling a bit worried about not being able to give a completely honest answer.

¶ I was—I think naturally—unhappy at Dovercourt but I was terrified to leave it. There were rumours that if you were lucky in your adoption the people might help your parents—but it was also said that girls of fifteen like myself were only wanted by English families as servants. What frightened me was the thought that I would be giving strangers absolute power over me. I didn't know if the Committee would still care what became of me once I had left the camp. I tried to find out but I didn't believe what I was told because naturally it was reassuring. Everybody wanted us to leave so that more children could be brought over from Germany. I can see now that the next step determined the whole of my life but I was made to feel very guilty about taking it with so much care.

¶ Every evening lists of names were read over the loudspeaker, of children who would be leaving the camp the following day. One night I heard my name. I had not expected it, I had to go to the office afterwards to find out what list it was on. I was to go to a boarding school in Manchester. I did not even know what the term boarding school meant.

¶ Prospective foster-parents were usually shown round at mealtimes, when we sat, boys and girls separately, according to age. The people walked down the rows of children, picking out this one or that, rather like a cattle market.

¶ In Germany I had never planned my future because everything was so uncertain, I had never dared to hope for a career—my schooling had been interrupted when I was thirteen. When I came to England I thought that now I would be like everyone else, that my life would be normal. When I was asked what I wanted to be I said a doctor. The woman who was filling the form in said: 'I can't put that down—you must remember that you are a refugee.'

A Soliloquy, December 22, 1938:

¶ *This must be Dovercourt—they've had much more snow than we have in London—not a taxi to be seen—nor anything else on the road —oh! now I know why, the road's like a skating rink—better keep to the path. 'How far is it to the holiday camp, please? About half an hour? Thanks.' Now I know what a leaden sea really looks like, I'd never seen one before. Goodness! What a wind along this sea front, it must be due east! That must be the camp—swimming bath and high diving-stage deep in snow—rows of wooden chalets, hundreds of them. Lovely in summer, but what hard luck to have this arctic spell just now! I suppose this big dance-hall place is where they all live in the daytime. What a noise!*

'Can I see the commandant please? I have a permit from the Central Committee to take back five girls to Bromley. You have boys here too, I see, brothers and sisters together. That's a good idea.'

Wherever shall I begin among these hundreds of children? Where's my list? (Don't fuss, this is not your business—in quietness and confidence—of course.) I must try to get the right children for all the good people at home, shall I ever remember all their instructions? Now I must make a start—how I hate treating people like things—it's like a slave market, Angles or angels—angels unawares. . . . 'Oh, thank you, Fräulein, it would be a help—yes, these three, brothers and sister, Karl (15), Theodore (14) and the fair-haired girl, Sonja (11), what a nice family group—from Vienna, did you say? Their father eingesperrt—oh, concentration camp. Yes, I must take them, I know where I can place them.'—'You want these two to come too, Karl? Cousins of yours, are they? Lisl and Silvio, sister and brother. Yes of course you want to be together, I think I can arrange it, not in the

*same house, but in the same town. Can you pack at once, children,
and meet me here in half an hour?'*

'*You want me to take these two, Fräulein? Eva and Rolf—they
have been in the camp three weeks? Why has nobody taken them
before? Oh, orphans, I see—too much responsibility! Well, I'll risk
it, I think I have the right home for them. No, children, you won't be
parted, cheer up, don't cry, I promise you shall be together.'*

*Now, to check up the list, that's seven, a three and a two and a
two—it's getting more complicated now. If only those two pianos
would stop for a moment, or play the same tune or play in time, so
that I could think! Now don't fuss!* '*You specially want me to take
this little one, Esther, do you, Fräulein, she is unhappy in this crowd,
and doesn't eat, well, yes, I can fit in a single one—can you pack
quickly, Esther.' Four o'clock already! The taxi will be here in ten
minutes!*

'*You want me to take Wolfgang, Fräulein? But my list is already
full! Oh, I think I can take him. Only one taxi, the other slithered
into a ditch! We must have another, but half my party is still
packing, scattered all over the camp. We must take the taxis back
for the next train. Now, who is crying over Wolfgang—is he your
brother, now don't upset him, don't cry so, Edith, I will try to find
a home for you near him later—('Inasmuch as ye did it not') Oh,
no, no, no! If you can pack quickly, Edith, you can come too, I will
find you a home somewhere. All right, Wolfgang, cheer up, she is
coming with you.'*

*Now the children are all here, where are the taxis? This is just
like the conventional nightmare when you miss one train after
another.* '*Please, Fräulein, send a telegram to this address. Say:
Bringing ten, arriving 9.30'. What will they say to that!*

'*Now children, if we don't catch this next train we can't get home
tonight, so keep together and stand by your suitcases.' At last!
Ten children, ten suitcases, and ten rucksacks. 'Auf Wiedersehen,
Fräulein, many thanks!'*

I

¶ *Our local Committee for the Care of Refugee Children from Germany was formed early in December 1938. Letters from the Mayor asking for help appeared in the local Press for several weeks, and there was an immediate response in the form of donations, invitations, and offers of education.*

From the beginning the Committee concentrated on requests for offers of hospitality for the children in private homes, either free or with a maintenance grant, which was fixed at the rate of 12s. 6d. weekly, the normal amount paid for boarded-out children in England. They resolved not to found Hostels for the children unless other means failed, realising that true home life was the necessity for happiness, and that the best interest of the children would be served by helping them to merge into the population as British citizens, rather than to isolate them in little foreign colonies.

¶ I was nine years old when I left Germany with my parents. A friend saw us off and even I knew that it was a terrible thing—not because we were going but because he was staying.

¶ My parents are both artists and we left Berlin in July 1933, when I was eleven. We first went to Paris. In 1937 my parents came to England. At that time I was at a German co-educational school in Switzerland. In 1938 I was sent to another school in Italy, but this was closed shortly afterwards by the government, as it was Jewish. I then made my way to Paris with the help of friends, and waited for a visa to England which came just before the war.

¶ Both my parents were doctors. We left Vienna in August 1938, and first went to Jugoslavia, to stay with an aunt, awaiting an American visa. In November 1938 my father was offered a place as one of the fifty Austrian doctors who were to be allowed to practise in England after a restricted course of two years. And so we came to London shortly before my ninth birthday.

¶ I came here at the age of five in July 1939. My parents are

Austrian Jews and had already been refugees in various countries for some years—Russia, Sicily, and finally Greece.

¶ My father was one of the first group to come to England, at the beginning of November 1938. As I was still under sixteen years of age, I qualified to travel as a child with my mother. We left Prague in a large and well organised transport, accompanied by British couriers, in the late evening of December 14th. My future wife was, unknown to me, on the same train. As we had to avoid passing through German territory, our journey to England had to be made through Poland, and thence by boat from Gdynia to London. On Christmas Eve, my mother and I were re-united with my father and many friends at one of the camps for refugees in Surrey.

¶ Emigration from our very small provincial place was difficult, it was impossible to be helped by the children's transport or similar organisations. We managed in the end, though in a very untidy manner and nearly lost my eldest sister who was over sixteen and so could not be registered on our parents' passport. She arrived just before the war, one day before her eighteenth birthday.

¶ At the frontier town of Aachen all Jews had to leave the train; all except myself were allowed to continue their journey. The reason for my being kept behind I can only guess at. I looked very 'Aryan' at the age of fourteen when my hair was still very light blonde. I was searched bodily by what seemed to me at the time an enormous woman and my few belongings were turned upside down. I can only imagine that they thought that my family were taking advantage of the fact that I looked so un-Jewish and was still a child, and were trying to smuggle valuables out of the country. Whatever the reason, they were certainly looking for something, and it was a harrowing and terrifying experience for a child. The lining of my new warm gloves was ripped open, so was a new manicure set I had just had as a farewell present from a friend. My chocolates were squashed, and so on. . . . Eventually I was allowed to leave, after the officers or guards or whatever they were had even perused my diary where I had vividly recorded my uncle's recent suicide, when the Gestapo came for him. I had secreted this in my case, naturally my parents would never have allowed me to take this, had they known. I now had to wait several hours for another train, then had to change trains in

Brussels. I must have looked a bit pathetic and forlorn and a Belgian porter came and talked to me in Yiddish, which I could just barely understand. He was very nice and helped me to get on the right train. The first 'human being' I had met since leaving my parents. Then later in England, I remember, I was quite sure that I was in the wrong, first-class compartment, when I found the seats upholstered, but by then I was too tired and exhausted to care. I arrived in London at Victoria station twelve hours late. My sister, who was meeting me there, was—not unnaturally—in a great state of agitation by then. I was so tired and dazed that I simply got out of the train and sat on my case on the platform, not even looking for her. My sister passed by me several times before realising it was me. She was now living in London, and had a little room in Euston. After cabling my arrival to my parents (I can guess what their state of mind must have been by then) we went by underground to her lodgings and I remember being greatly alarmed by the black uniforms of the underground guards, which reminded me of SS uniforms.

¶ There were five of us—the youngest was not yet two and I was fourteen. We had relations in England and my mother travelled back and forth, rather like a mother-cat transferring her kittens, and parked us wherever she could. The whole thing was so haphazard that the family who looked after one of my sisters took steps to adopt her. As soon as possible my mother went round collecting us up again.

¶ My half-sister was already in England and managed to obtain a 'Trainee Permit' for me, enabling me to stay for twelve months. The war started before then. . . . I was fifteen years old.

¶ My name was included in a children's transport because a friend of mine who worked in Bloomsbury House added it without permission so that when I arrived in London no organisation felt responsible for me. I was therefore immediately made to act like a grown-up, a situation I was ludicrously unequal to. My friend from home, a refugee like myself and also totally without money, found me a place in Hampstead as an au pair. I was sixteen years old.

¶ I came to England to live under the guardianship of a curate of the Church of England. He was in his mid-thirties and a bachelor and had seen my photograph displayed somewhere and taken pity. I was then ten years old.

¶ I was nearly eleven when I came to England accompanied by my sister, then aged four and a half. We spent one night in London with an aunt who had arrived a little sooner, then we immediately went to our foster-parents. This young couple had originally asked for one refugee child, but apparently when they saw a photo of my sister and me they felt they did not want to part sisters and so asked for both of us.

¶ My father's sister had emigrated to England. At a public meeting she decided to sit down next to the only other woman as stout as herself, and discovered that she intended to deal with the problem of non-Aryan Christian children by opening a home for twelve of them, and 'booked' two places for my sister and me, though we were rather older than the children she had had in mind.

¶ My father was a minister of the Lutheran church, and had come to England to escape being sent to a concentration camp. But in January 1939 he decided that he and my mother must return to Germany; they left myself and my sister, as being old enough to be corrupted by the régime, to be cared for in England, She was seven and I was nine years old.

¶ I came to England at the age of fifteen, seven days before the war. On arrival it was discovered that my sister should have come instead. I was nearly sent back, but it was too close to the war. My sister perished at Auschwitz.

¶ I came from Berlin via Holland—we were on our way to Chile when our ship struck a mine and we were landed in England by the boat that picked us up. I was eleven years old.

¶ *In May 1940, a few days after the Nazis had invaded Holland, a coal barge landed in Liverpool from Amsterdam. She had 140 passengers on board, amongst them 60 children, all refugees from Germany and all without parents or relatives. These had been living at a children's refugee hostel in Amsterdam, and been taken to the Amsterdam harbour a few hours before the German troops occupied the town. They had been dive-bombed by German planes, but there had been no casualties. Still, the Nazis claimed later to have sunk it. Luckily, the Chairman of the Manchester Refugee Committee, invited by the B.B.C. Overseas Service, could broadcast their safe arrival in England. The children were between eleven and sixteen years old.*

II

¶ I hated leaving home, the decision was fairly suddenly sprung on me, but even at the age of ten I realised that I was coming to a place where I would no longer have to be frightened.

¶ It was not until the train pulled in at Liverpool Street Station and we were met by our 'uncle' and 'aunt' that I felt just a little excited and conscious of the fact that the journey was over; that I was with strange people in a strange land, my mother would not be there to tuck me up in bed, and the house I was going to was just a house and not a home. But I did not feel sad. It was like being on holiday; everything was new and exciting and the sense of fear and hurry—which I'd almost grown accustomed to—left me for the first time that night. I was seven years old.

¶ At Harwich we were loaded on to trains without much delay. The English trains seemed strange to us; we had always travelled on wooden seats; and funniest of all, children were running along the corridors showing everyone their newest discovery—the English toilet paper, hard and shiny. At Liverpool Street Station we all had to enter a large Drill Hall which had been turned into a reception centre. I had no idea what would happen to my brother and me. Many children were met immediately by relatives or taken straight off to other centres. We just sat and sat, too tired and miserable to say much. Eventually I heard our name being called and there was our sponsor, who had come specially to London to meet us. It seemed good to have somebody to belong to and to have the responsibility of my seven-year-old brother partially lifted off my shoulders. I was fourteen years old.

¶ I can remember the Customs examination at Harwich, and then the wearisome waiting in a cavernous electrically lit hall somewhere on Liverpool Street Station. My guarantor, a spinster lady in her forties, was there with her brother to take me home in his little car. She was a Unitarian and would have adopted me and become fully responsible for me if my parents had not survived. She was very relieved to find that I already knew some English, since she knew little German. I was seven years old.

¶ Those who had relatives or friends to go to were taken to the Great Eastern Hotel to await their escorts. They were the lucky few. . . . I had an aunt here in England and also my Granny and indeed they came to meet me, but they themselves were in no position to take me into their charge. So I waited with the unclaimed. At last a number of us were taken back to the station and were put on a special train to a hostel. I was eleven years old.

¶ At Liverpool Street we sat in another waiting room, for what seemed like many hours, but there was a great difference from the one where we had said our last good-byes. Here there was no crying and no grief. A disciplined silence prevailed, interrupted only by the calling of our numbers to be collected by our guarantors. There was nothing familiar, nothing reassuring, and I think at that moment many of us would gladly have exchanged our newly won freedom for the grief-stricken waiting-room where we were still at home and not alone. I was sixteen years old when I came.

¶ I was seven years two months, and my sister exactly a year older, on the day we arrived in England, tired, under-nourished, and frightened. The labels hanging round our necks did little to help us look appealing. We had to walk in file up the platform and line up to be photographed by newspaper cameramen. I do not remember any of the formalities that undoubtedly did go on, just that we were in a room facing a man and a woman and were told that they were Mr. and Mrs. Smith (referred to from now on as Uncle and Aunt). They put us in their car and we set off to drive some miles to their home. We sat in the back, my sister and I, clutching hands, tired with all that had gone before, and confused with all the babble of English that we had heard of which we could understand not a word.

¶ At Harwich we were met by two English ladies and about a dozen of us were put into their charge, to go on to Norwich. I remember a draughty place (a railway waiting-room, perhaps?) and my first sight of an open coal fire, which was lovely when one stood in front of it, but not much use across the room. On our way from Harwich to Norwich we were being taught to say 'How do you do?'. We had great difficulty in saying, 'Quite well, thank you'. Only one of these ladies could speak German, and she was bewildered, I expect, by our volubility and Viennese accent. There was one boy who displayed a whole Salami sausage. One of the ladies smelled it and must have thought that it was bad, because she threw it out of the window before he could stop her and make himself understood.

¶ The boat and train journey were very frightening to me as I had never been away from my mother before. I remember being in a large bare hall on arrival in England and sitting on chairs with the other children waiting for the new parents who were to care for them. I had always been sad that I did not have a very young mother like other children of my own age and one of the things I regret most in my life is that I often said to my mother that I wished this. It must have been very hurtful to her, especially since on looking at her photograph I can see that she was not so very old at all. I think one should be careful what one wishes in life, since it turned out that my foster mother was indeed very young and very lovely. I was seven years old when I arrived.

¶ After a rest in the hotel room in Bloomsbury where our guarantors had stayed, we had a quick sight-seeing tour of London, of which I remember nothing, and a visit to the Houses of Parliament which I remember very well. I was fourteen years old when I came.

¶ I was ten years old when I arrived and found it difficult to accept that life in England was 'normal', that one could walk in the street, go into a shop or get on to a bus without fear of attack or insult.

III

¶ *A boy whom I befriended at Dovercourt said to me: 'I have a girl cousin of sixteen on my mother's side who wants to come to England and cannot come through the Children's Movement because they cannot take any more. Can you take her?' I told him we would have to think it over. He was most insistent, telling us what a good girl she was, and how we would love her and she'd love us. And would we be coming across next Wednesday as well as on Sunday so that he could write and let his people know? He would send for her photograph so that we could see how nice she was, etc. He certainly left no stone unturned. She arrived at Claydon one Friday night in July 1939. We arranged for her cousin to take charge of her until we went for her the following Sunday. We thought a day or so with her cousin would help to settle her in a strange land. We drove up to London to collect her and right from the start we knew we would love her, and although naturally at first she was a little quiet, by the time we arrived home, prolonging the journey by a tour of the Essex countryside and tea at an Old World Cottage, she was one of us.*

¶ There was a boy of three or four in our transport who continually repeated a name and address. After we had left Germany he asked me to write it down. They were people in England who might help his parents.

¶ When I arrived I told everyone about my anxieties for my parents and asked them to help. But they were always so reassuring that after quite a short time of living in England I began to believe that my parents had nothing to fear. I was thirteen years old.

¶ My sister had a job in Woburn House and managed to get a domestic permit for our mother and also managed, heaven knows how, to find a guarantor for our father, who was already over sixty. I still have in my possession the cable we received from our parents 'Arriving Croydon Airport Wednesday 6th September.' On Monday war broke out—we had lost the race by three days. My sister phoned our parents when war was imminent and urged them to try and get out anywhere they could get to. They couldn't get a plane before the sixth, didn't want to risk being parted and obviously still hoped they would be permitted to leave. We received the usual Red Cross messages after that for a couple of years, then they stopped. After the war we learned that they had shared the fate of six million others.

¶ I knew that I ought to badger Bloomsbury House about my sister. I knew it while I rummaged about at Foyle's and Bumpus, while I stared incredulously at the incredible Amusement Arcades and Funlands along Charing Cross Road and Oxford Street, while I watched performance after performance at the local cinema, for 3d., under the pretence of wanting to learn English. I had always been pathologically shy of offices and officials. The knowledge of having to go to an office used to torture me for days in advance. Now my shyness was aggravated by the strange monster city, so foreign too, so far from my sister that it could not possibly be interested in her or in me. I had asked diffidently, soon after my arrival, had received a hasty reply and had given up. I made my next attempt three weeks later. I had been invited by a committee lady to my first English tea. I asked. She said she would try. It was too late. Since then the suspicion has remained that for my office neurosis my sister had to pay an exorbitant price—the forced labour camp and Auschwitz.

¶ *It is a haunting sorrow to me that there were children we were corresponding about and trying to get hospitality for up to the last minute, some in particular who should have been on the transport that was cancelled at the last minute, and for whom we made so many efforts after war started to get them out through other countries, but ultimately failed and we can only assume what their fate was.*

NEW HOMES

I

¶ My parents and I arrived in London with, I think it was, ten shillings each. We lived with an aunt in three pretty awful rooms and seemed to exist on stews made of dried prunes, apple-slices, dried apricot etc. I was sent to school on the Monday following the Friday of our arrival. I could just speak and understand enough English not to be entirely lost. The teacher was nice and I got very childish readers in order to improve my English. Although I could see that my parents were very unhappy at this time, I was all right. I was nine years old.

¶ My parents and I tramped around Swiss Cottage, hoping that some opening would occur for earning our living. It was a mixture of idyll and depression. Idyll: lots of leisure, lots of reading, talking, walking, a certain amount of sight-seeing, friends and relatives visiting us and inviting us or taking us out in their cars—never before or since have I had so many car-rides! They were kind, hospitable, and tried to help—but they obviously hadn't the means to support us, and there was no way of getting round the bar on paid work. Depression: the hopelessness of this situation. We would get gifts, or loans, or somebody would sell something, or a relative abroad repaid a debt—anyway, we lived from day to day, week to week, according to how the odd, quite unpredictable amounts of money happened to come in. I was then fourteen years old.

¶ My parents and I lived for three weeks in a hostel in London's East End—a horror that is unforgettable. So much unhappy humanity in one place, no one caring about anyone else—someone even stole two of our suitcases and we had arrived with little enough. Eventually we found a furnished room and in July of that year we were able to bring my brother over from Holland. Our landlady allowed my brother to stay on the understanding that he clean the house every Friday. Often, that first winter, we sat in my parents' bed to keep warm. Every week my father queued up at Woburn House for his week's allowance

—which often ran out before more money was due. But we were happy, we were free, we were together, we were human again. . . . I was then twelve years old.

¶ My parents arrived with me in England with the proverbial few pounds in their pockets and the idea of going on to a cousin in America. However, our visas were twice cancelled and by the time there was another opportunity we had already dug some roots in this country. For the first few months we lived in one small room. Only my mother was allowed to work; she had a job as a machinist. On the outbreak of war my father was interned on the Isle of Man. My mother and I were evacuated to a small village in Buckinghamshire. The people we stayed with there were very kind but I turned rather difficult, not wanting to go to school to learn English, refusing the food given. Indeed from being a friendly, extrovert child I turned into something more of an obstinate introvert. However, this was just a phase. It was at this time that we got into the habit of speaking only English in case people should think we were talking about them. Subsequently my parents used to speak German to each other but not in my presence as I hated being 'different' even whilst realising all the time that somehow I was. I was five years old when I came.

¶ My parents had to leave everything behind in Germany, their life savings and our home, and my mother was only allowed to come to this country as a domestic servant and worked for several years in a hostel as cook to twenty refugee boys. My father was not allowed to take proper employment at the time, but helped with odd jobs in the hostel. Later my parents were interned on the Isle of Man for six months. I was eleven years old when we came.

¶ Looking back, I get the impression that the couple who took us in did it for selfish reasons. My mother did all the work of the house to allow the wife much free time. Mother was called plain *Frau*—no name! I wasn't given any sweets as their own children were, at first she was not given a stamp for letters home and, of course, had no money to buy anything with as she had no work-permit. I was eight years old.

¶ In Germany my parents had belonged to what might be called the upper middle class among the local Jews. Since we left it very late before deciding to emigrate they had to leave behind practically all their belongings as well as property, and from 1939 to 1945 we carried on a pretty desperate struggle for existence, depending for bare financial support on the generosity of relatives in the U.S.A. My father, after having been for a short while in Dachau, suffered also a period of internment by the British as an enemy alien. He was for a long time denied a labour permit, and had to perform menial jobs such as clearing debris from bombed sites in the City of London quite out of keeping with his training, intelligence, and social background. All these trials, plus the hazards of bombing and living in war-time Britain with my grandmother in very poor accommodation led my mother to attempt suicide. Fortunately she was un-successful. I was seven years old when we came.

¶ I had felt in Berlin that all was not well with my parents' marriage, but my father was nearly always away on business trips and my mother always looked after me and lived her own life. Owing to the fact that in London we were suddenly forced to live together at very close quarters my parents quarrelled constantly. My father was a very hard worker, and I suppose felt very bitter that everything had been taken from him by the Nazis, and my mother being a very soft and dependent person found it increasingly difficult to follow my father in his perpetual drive to work harder and harder. I felt very much in the middle of this and my loyalties were torn. My one desire was to go to university, but my father simply would not con-sider this, and said that it was my duty to start work at once, and contribute to the household. I was sixteen years old.

¶ My parents obtained permission to leave Czechoslovakia and reached England about a month after me, at the end of July, 1939. By this time I could no longer speak proper German and my mother had to interpret for my father when he wanted to speak to me. They lived in a horrible boarding house where the landlady gave them to understand that she was keeping them out of charity whereas in fact the Refugee Committee was paying her quite well. Later my parents had a room in a Vic-torian house which had been taken over as a refugee hostel (I think by the Quakers); I was given a room of my own to sleep in which had previously been the dressing-room attached to the principal bedroom; this was occupied by an extremely pious Jew and his even more pious blonde convert wife and their young baby. I cannot remember the baby ever crying, but the father's Hebrew sing-song prayers are a very vivid memory. This was the time of the air-raids; we had plenty of bombs, though I cannot remember ever being positively frightened. My idea was that God had taken so much trouble to get us to England that He wouldn't waste it all by letting us be bombed. I was seven years old when I came.

¶ In England, my mother's twin sister met me and I lived with her and her family. I hated England, refused to learn English, I always thought the teacher was cross with me because I did not understand. Six months later my mother and father came over penniless. Suddenly I spoke English, and for many years it was as if I had never known German. More than anything in the world I wanted to be an English girl; I rejected my past and my parents. As I grew up I was paralysed with shyness, petrified in case my parents should come to school and that my friends should hear them speak with their broken accents. Their speech and their ways were different and I suffered. I was seven years old when I came.

¶ My aunt who looked after us was rather a nervous type who managed to have an unsettling effect on children and adults alike. She was nervous about how to feed us, about how to bring us up. . . . My uncle was a very much calmer sort of person, but he had to travel to his hat factory every day and never seemed to be in the house for very long. They had two children, a daughter and a son who were a few years older than my brother and I—old enough, for the son at least, to lord it over us whenever the opportunity presented itself. Then there was my brother, just eighteen months older than me—I was seven when we came—who teased and bullied me rather more cruelly and frequently than he had done at home. As for my parents, they were not around to comfort me. What was worse, perhaps, I had no particular longing to see them; their marriage had not been a success from the start and to witness their quarrelling was an upsetting experience I was glad to have left behind. When they arrived in March 1939 I regarded the event as a mixed blessing. Of course it was a relief to see them safe and well, but I saw them now as foreigners and intruders. I objected to the Salami sandwiches made with German bread which they'd specially saved for me. I'd only just got used to English toast, marmalade, and grapefruit for breakfast. And it wasn't just my imagination that they brought a new tension into the household; the nerves of my aunt grew appreciably tauter as she had more guests to deal with, and understandably so. From the start she did not hit it off with my mother, who was herself in a nervous state. And I, never a very strong or thick-skinned person, became increasingly nervous in my own introverted way. I started having asthma attacks. At first they were passed off as little more than bronchitis. But as the months passed they grew increasingly severe and more frequent. My absence from school did not help to improve my confidence or my knowledge of English. Nevertheless I managed to divest myself of the remaining shreds of my German past. Just the passing of time helped. Getting rid of the last of my German clothes was both symbolic and a practical gesture. As I gained confidence I went out more and more on my own and so did not have to put up with the loud foreign ways of my parents and relatives. I even began to dream in English. But my parents—through no fault of their own—were a constant inhibiting factor. My father was of course refused permission to practise as a doctor; the threat of his being ordered to one of the internment camps was always present, and for many weeks he failed to find work of any sort. The knowledge that my father was without money rather spoiled the feeling of security I'd gained from the threepence pocket money which my aunt gave me each week. In the summer of 1940 we heard that there was now no possibility of our emigrating to America—a hope that we'd kept alive ever since we'd booked a passage to New York before even coming to England. We also had news from Hamburg that our 'lift'—containing all our possessions except what we brought over by hand, as well as £2,000 worth of medical equipment—had been destroyed in an R.A.F. raid. About this time too my father lost his job as a waiter in Lyons' Corner House and came to try his hand at teaching at the school which we were attending. In the spring of 1941 my father at last found a job which enabled him (and us) to become independent of our relatives. He was accepted as a locum doctor in Birmingham and a few months later we joined him there: a new house, a new school—and always the feeling that wherever we arrived and settled down we'd soon be on the move again.

¶ After the fall of France my father, who had been living in Paris at the time, escaped to England, landing at Plymouth.

Here he joined the British Army, but was soon invalided out of it, and came to live near us. He was penniless, and we used the pocket money which our guardians gave us to buy him a few basic things like handkerchiefs and cigarettes. Then he got a job as nightwatchman in a fashionable hotel, and in the daytime he tried to re-establish his old textile business. In the meantime the three of us had taken rooms in a boarding house in the attempt to have some sort of home together, but it didn't work out. When my sister left school she went to London to train as a nurse; soon after, my father set up business in London. I went back to my former foster-home. By the end of the war my father had made enough money to repay our guardians. I was twelve years old when I came.

¶ I was six years old when I came and my mother followed just before the war. I stayed with foster parents and found it impossible to love two people as my mother. At first, my own mother's visits and especially her departures were an agony. Gradually, as my foster mother took over my affections—and I welcomed this—my own mother's visits were still an agony but now because of the guilt feelings they aroused in me.

¶ I was thirteen years old when I came. Although my father was in England, for a large part of the time we were never in the same place at the same time. When we were, there was a lot of friction, due in part to the fact that my mother had been my favourite parent, and I probably resented having him here instead of her.

¶ I was ten years old when I came. My mother was here but I only saw her about once a year—there wasn't money for my fare.

¶ I was fourteen years old when I came. My father's (and our) dependence on other people for our very livelihood converted my relationship of obedience into one of partnership even more quickly and radically than would have happened as the result of ordinary growing up.

¶ I was six years old when I came and as I grew older my feelings towards my parents were a mixture of pity for their disabilities and resentment at the handicaps—social and economic—imposed on me as a result of having refugee parents.

¶ I was eleven years old when I came. My parents didn't have the social standing they would have had in Germany, but I never minded saying that my father was a factory worker, because I could introduce him and I felt that people would know what he is.

II

From Inge's Diary (translated)

¶ I am twelve years old and have come with my sister to live in the house of Mr. and Mrs. Roberts. We have a governess, an English Miss (like in a book). Mr. and Mrs. Roberts are very upset because she told them that I am lazy and don't learn English as well as I could. If I knew English life would be easy!

Yesterday evening in bed I remembered how I had prayed to God to send me to England. Well—He granted my wish. And now I lie in bed and pray that I may soon be allowed to return to my parents, to Vienna without Hitler. Vienna is my home and I shall always remain a Viennese at heart.

When my parents found fault with me, which happened quite often, I took it to heart and thought: it's for the whole of my life. But when people in a strange country (and strangers) find fault, I immediately think the worst—that they want to bully me, don't like me, etc. When they say to us: 'Take your coats, it's cold,' I feel that this isn't said out of love for me but so that they don't lay themselves open to criticism, because they are responsible.

Mrs. Roberts said: 'We give you a home, and you must keep it nice,' and I thought: and if we don't keep it nice you won't give us a home?

When I laugh I suddenly think: What have I got to laugh about? How frantically I envy other children who are able to be together with their parents. To be in a foreign country is a punishment to me! When I am dead they will have to put on my grave that here lies a child who died of homesickness.

Today Mr. Roberts told me that he would send me to an institution if I wouldn't speak English. It is only recently that I have come to love my mother-tongue above everything else. I have never had this feeling about it before. Here, everybody speaks English, from babies to grandfathers. It hurts me to hear it. And when I hear or read German somewhere, it makes my heart beat faster. . . .

Where is my good temper, where is my sense of humour, my

ability to enjoy life? Everything is gone. I don't care about anything—except being together again with my family. Then nothing would matter. God should have protected me from the days I am living through now.

My friend is here with her parents, and she is homesick too —for Vienna. She is homesick once and I am doubly homesick.

I have had a terrible scare, because—I can hardly write it down—because if I start going to school here perhaps I shall have to continue until I am old enough to leave. I thought that I had come here for a year. Now Mr. Roberts says that we would take the exam to enter school perhaps only next summer, because I still know so little English. Next summer one year will be up! They must think three to five years. Or perhaps even longer. But after the first year they will no longer have a strong, healthy child.

Yesterday we were talking about Germany. Mr. Roberts asked Lieselotte: 'Didn't you have anything to eat any more?' Lieselotte: 'Oh, it wasn't as bad as that. Only, no butter, no meat, no fruit and no milk. But enough to live on.' 'Then why did you come to England?' (This might have been interpreted as a reproach, but he said it unsuspectingly and of course he meant all Jews.) 'But we couldn't live there—haven't you heard about 10th November? We couldn't go into a park, a theatre, or use a tram. In the street, anybody could do what they liked to us, the men were being imprisoned, we were thrown out of our homes.' 'Oh, I see.' He found it impossible to understand, but looked very sad and seemed to be taking it to heart. He said: 'I expected to find you very nervous, my wife and I were surprised that you weren't.' (I must say he is at times a little tactless.) But soon we were talking about something else. I know, only someone who has been through it can understand, and to be honest, I wouldn't be able to understand it either.

Today I saw a letter from Mutti to Mr. Roberts lying open on the table and I read it. And in it it said something like this: I am glad that you like Lieselotte so much, and I hope the same will soon be the case with Inge, who is a happy, jolly child (was it, once).

A relative has been visiting. She gave us sixpence and Lieselotte asked if we could accept it. Mrs. Roberts said: 'Of course, you are her adopted nieces.' That means in other words that we are her adopted CHILDREN. That is very nice of them but please, Mr. and Mrs. Roberts, don't say it, it hurts me almost as much as if you were to say 'we hate these children'. We are not your children, no, no, never!

III

¶ Even as a boy of twelve I knew that being taken in by a family instead of going to a hostel or institution of some kind was not only preferable, but one step up in the social scale. I had stayed with a family for a few days in transit to a hostel, but this family asked if I wanted to stay with them, and of course I was only too glad. The family consisted of an elderly couple and a single daughter in her early thirties and they did everything they could to make me feel a part of their family circle. Mr. and Mrs. R. were devoutly religious, comfortably off, were kind, sympathetic, had themselves had six children, and though perhaps narrow in the cultural sense (theatre and films were never mentioned) enjoyed social life through the church which they encouraged me to join (my father was a converted Jew). They were in fact a truly charming and genuine family. It was not their fault that I found their life a little restrictive, a little lonely and lacking in any expression of affection, though without doubt I felt secure with them, they never made me feel as if I were a burden to them and seemed to grow fond of me and I certainly of them. They were kind, quite unselfish, anxious to make me feel one of them, though I never quite got over the feeling of being a guest. Particularly the first year I would never dare to ask for a second helping—unless they asked me first—fearing that I might prove too expensive for them. Their house was large and desperately cold in winter, and Sundays were Victorian, very sedate and often a little boring, but their faith was very real and quite inspiring. I felt quite guilty not being able to live up to it. They taught me many things in matters of taste (in literature and music) and, most important, they taught me to become English.

¶ As a girl of ten I was taken into a wonderful foster home. I was terribly happy there and still remember this period with joy. I could hardly remember my parents being as young and carefree and gay as this lovely couple I had come to.

¶ These people were simply marvellous—if standards of human decency and ordinary down-to-earth kindness are the measurements by which we judge them. These relatively simple people did not allow their traditional doubt about Jews or their current hate of Germans to deter them from taking into their modest homes us foreign-speaking and strangely dressed youngsters.

¶ There was the loneliness of being surrounded entirely by strange sights and sounds; the feeling of helplessness brought on by not being able to communicate one's smallest wants to people who were willing to help but did not speak your language; and the suspicion engendered by the thought that those very people might not recognise you as a fellow human being but regard you as a refugee, and condemn you as an enemy of their country. In a boy of eight years, all these feelings were exaggerated and added up to one overriding emotion: bewilderment.

¶ At the time, as a boy of fourteen, I was probably not aware of the magnitude of the adjustment that faced me and I saw the transfer from one country to another as an adventure which I welcomed eagerly. This attitude was reinforced by the desire to get away from Germany and all her horrors and to forget about it as quickly as possible by becoming English. My command of the English language was slight on arrival, yet I can hardly remember now a transitional period of becoming gradually more proficient. I suddenly seemed to be able to speak and write English fluently. I do, however, remember being taught a lot of knowhow about the English way of life, mainly by the doctor's wife with whom I stayed.

¶ I was taken by a Jewish family in London, and my sister went to another Jewish family; she was seven and I was eight years old. We were both treated extremely well and with great kindness. Both families saw to it that we were able to be together as often as possible. We were not lonely as both families had children of their own round about our age, and we were busy learning English and being absorbed into English life, which is certainly different to the general continental way of living. I remember writing home to Germany: the windows are different, the light switches, the food, the way the beds are made, school hours. . . .

¶ I was desperately unhappy in the first foster home to which I went as a girl of eleven. The people didn't understand me at

all and the home was so different from my own. They meant
well, no doubt, but it was not a success and they realised it too,
for I was taken from them and this time I was moved to a young
married couple. This home was more familiar, but again I was
there only a short time. Looking back I suppose I must have
been a very difficult child. I can't remember being disobedient
particularly, but something must have been drastically wrong.
I came from a home and although one may call it broken (my
parents were divorced) it was a home none the less where I was
much loved and spoiled. I had everything I wanted but my father
was also very strict—he stood no nonsense—hence I had security.
Now all this was gone in a flash.

¶ I came to a Vicarage in Essex as a girl of fourteen. They expected a lot of work from me, especially the Vicar's wife. I had
to ask for stamps, for shoe repair, etc. and it took all my courage
to do so for money was tight. I was never refused these items
but made to feel it all the same. I loved to go to church (I was
brought up a Lutheran), my only spare time and also contact
with some other people. After the fall of France Essex became
a defence zone and I was moved. The second family gave me
2s. 6d. pocket money, which was a real help.

¶ I went to my first foster home as a boy of eleven, together
with my cousin. Two incidents stand out in my mind about our
brief stay. One was the lady's insistence that she should bathe
us, which very much offended my modesty. The other—on
Sunday she took us to church and just as soon as I realised
where we were going I protested strongly shouting loudly 'Jude,
Jude'. Not understanding what I said, the lady thought that I
was ill and called for a doctor. I was confined to bed and as I
could hardly be left on my own there was no church for any of
us that day.

¶ I lived for five years with an English family who had one
son. I had been an only daughter deeply attached to my parents
and the break at the age of eleven was a difficult one. I think
I was probably a difficult foster child—I do however remember
wanting very much to be part of the family with whom I lived
but I never felt this. I deeply resented my loss of education as
I had just started a higher education in Prague and I felt that I
was never given a true opportunity in this way. Besides the loss
of my parents, this, when younger, was my greatest resentment.

¶ The family to which I went as a boy of thirteen was a young couple with a baby daughter. They lived in a semi-detached house in a Glasgow suburb and owned a chemist's shop in a slum area. I must have been quite a handful! I had been brought up to expect it as natural that I should go to school until I was eighteen and then to University—it had been so drilled into me as a pre-ordained career that the existence of other possibilities never entered my mind. They were not prepared for this and aghast that anybody should expect them to pay out that sort of money to a perfect stranger. I stayed with them for only about two months.

¶ As a girl of fourteen I was taken in by a family in the East End of London. Looking back now I realise that they were very kind, generous, and well-meaning people. At the time it was for me rather shattering. They lived in a tiny terrace house in a dreadful little road. There was a workroom at the back where some sort of tailoring work was done. There was no bathroom and I shared a bed with one of the daughters. We washed in the sink in the kitchen or went to a Public Bath. I had never seen such conditions and so felt rather awful. I went to evening classes to learn English—years later I was to teach Drama in the same school.

¶ I was very happy both in the foster home and in the school I attended. Unfortunately the husband made mildly amorous advances to me one evening, which I confided to his daughter. This, a few days later, resulted in my dramatic eviction. I was thirteen: a short, stocky, somewhat busty child and—after my dismissal from this household—a very badly dressed one: my clothes somehow got left behind.

¶ I was sixteen years old when I came and partially blind, and this made life more difficult in new surroundings. There was the problem of seeing the children safely across the road, being sent to the shops and not seeing which was the right one to go into; the bumping into lamp-posts and falling into man-holes had somehow been more bearable at home than it was among these strange people. I expect my guarantors were really very patient with me, they had heard of the novelty of bringing over a refugee girl as a mother's help, they had hoped to get a sort of maid, which I was only too willing to be, but they had not reckoned with my disability, or with my emotional problems, or with my anxieties for my parents. They had never heard of Vienna, only very vaguely about us refugee children, they had never before met a Jew face to face.

¶ I was in a foster home for a time as a boy of sixteen. What I have never been able to forget or forgive was the discrimination. I was given margarine when the rest of the family ate butter, on only one slice of bread was I allowed to put jam—the very jam for which I had collected the brambles. When visitors came I was banished to the kitchen where I also had my meals. My position was somewhere between that of a poor relative and a domestic servant, without the privileges of the one or the rights of the other.

¶ I was a girl of nine when my foster parents took me into their home in a Railway Company cottage—Uncle worked on the railways. Aunty had had a child many years before, but it had died soon after birth, and she had never had another. I think that my arrival had been anticipated with some excitement, and on being shown my bedroom, I remember the thrill of opening drawers to find them crammed with brand new toys, dolls, books, etc. As the days passed, I do not think I was really homesick but took great delight in discovering things that were new to me, the most fascinating of which were the open fires, and when I thought that no one was watching, I would put piece upon piece of paper on the fire just for the sheer joy of watching it burn. My home life had its ups and downs. My aunt and uncle were fond of me in their way but had no real understanding of a child's needs and often I would feel very lonely as I did not have any other children to play with. They tended to be rather possessive, but things improved as I grew older and when I was about fourteen I joined Youth Clubs, etc., and made quite a number of good friends, whom I was always allowed to invite home.

¶ I went into a foster home as a girl of seven. When my American visa came through the Germans had several times sunk ships carrying children to America and so my uncle (who was no relation at all) refused to let me go and indeed I lived with them for the next twenty years! When their own son was born I was eighteen but still living with them and it made no difference at all to their treatment of me, and I was never in any way made to feel that the coming of their own child lessened their affection for me. I did not leave home to live in a flat until I was twenty-nine, and even then I frequently went home for the week-ends. And even after my marriage I go to visit them frequently.

¶ I saw my guardian occasionally before she died. She grew to be very old. She sometimes blamed herself for not having treated me better. 'I expect I was difficult too,' I answered once. She brightened immediately, 'You *were*,' she said.

IV

¶ *In an endeavour to find the necessary available homes, I visited many rural communities. . . . It was a melancholy, heartbreaking experience. I was offered financial assistance, but rarely a home. Many more children could have been rescued if more Jewish homes had been placed at our disposal.*

—A Social Worker

¶ *Hospitality was offered by all sections of the community—a questionnaire was drawn up for the use of the organisations in Germany. There were insufficient offers of orthodox Jewish homes for the number of orthodox parents applying in Germany. The Movement had to notify the Reichsvertretung that a certain number of orthodox children had to be held back from a special transport.*

A Great Adventure, Bloomsbury House, July 1944.

¶ *We now have six Roman Catholics and ten Protestants; the remaining thirty-two, who are listed as Jewish, are scattered about the county and it is not easy to get at them for instruction. Only three children are definitely receiving it, while three, backed up by the guardians, have definitely declared that they do not want it. Among the remainder there is a general tendency, supported in every case by the approval of parents or near relatives, to postpone decision, and study both Jewish and Christian outlook. Our invariable principle is that each child shall be treated as an individual, and that no child's conscience shall become a battle ground.*

Contemporary Report of local Refugee Committee.

¶ *When I was twelve years old my parents gave a home to a refugee girl of fourteen. I longed to comfort her and felt desperately sorry for her but being Jewish she could not somehow communicate with us. My mother and father were prepared to be sympathetic and maybe they did help her—but I used to wish so desperately that I*

too was Jewish because she couldn't seem to see that we did under-
stand. On balance I should say I have gained a lot from having her
as a sister. It has made me think about religion, race and family
relations, and I have developed an unorthodox outlook on life.

¶ It seems that although my uncle and aunt made no effort
whatever to give me any special religious training of any kind,
they bore in mind my Jewish origins and during all my life with
them I always seem to have known some Jewish people.

¶ As a girl of fifteen I went into a non-Jewish foster home together with my brother, aged twelve, and my little sister, aged
eight. We came from an orthodox background. I can still hear
the taunts of 'Your own don't want you, so we took you in.' They
received payment for our keep. I did the work, and later worked
full time, handing in my wages intact, as did my brother at
fourteen. The Refugee Committee did on rare occasions come
to see us. 'Well, how are you, my dear?' (This in *their* presence,
in a nice, comfortable room.) 'I can see you are well looked after
here. Do you need any clothes? No, I can see they keep you all
well dressed.' The thought never seemed to occur to the visitor
that we paid for all our clothes. And so she went happily on her
way, unaware of the silent heartbreak. Sometime we did have
contact with a Jewish family, as, for example, when the Jewish
Refugee Committee remembered us on *Pesach*,* and we were
asked to join in the *Seder*† celebrations with a Jewish family. I
remember the rare occasions when we were allowed to go to
Shul.‡ Not one of the congregation ever took an interest in us
or asked us home.

¶ As a girl of nine I went to foster parents who were members
of the Church of England, and from then on my Jewish faith
seemed to recede further and further from my mind. They made
no attempt to influence me—from an early age I had to decide
for myself. When I was a child, two local Jewish families befriended me and always made a point of inviting me to their
homes on special Jewish festival days. However, gradually I
seemed to lose touch with them, and over the years became
closer to the C. of E.

* Passover
† Eve of Passover
‡ Synagogue
3

¶ As a girl of eight I went with my younger sister into the home of Christadelphians and we were taught Bible knowledge and Christian behaviour by precept and example. All during the war and our difficult beginnings and readjustments the Roman Catholic representatives completely ignored us. We were only quarter Jewish and Uncle had obtained my father's permission to bring us up in their religious beliefs, when we first came to England.

¶ As a girl of six I went into a Christian family, the father being an English master in a Grammar school and a conscientious objector. The transition from being a Jew to being a Christian—and I am now a convinced Christian and a member of a church—was not difficult. My adoptive parents attended church regularly, prayed and taught me at home so that I grew up in this atmosphere and imbibed it. Their religion was a mixture of intellect and spirituality, so that when I questioned there were reasoned answers for me to accept or reject. My own mother visited us regularly during my childhood and youth, but we never discussed Judaism, so that there was no problem for me here.

¶ I was twelve years old when I came and during the war my father persuaded my sister and myself to be baptised 'for the sake of our children'. I was baptised when I was about sixteen. It seems rather unnecessary now. . . . People don't usually ask whether you were baptised—they ask who you are.

¶ I came as a girl of nine and shared my foster home, a vicarage, with two other Jewish refugee girls. The Jewish Children's Committee tried on several occasions to remove us to a Jewish hostel. We fought like mad to stay and were eventually left alone. Having at last found some security in our lives we were reluctant to give it up. I was fourteen when we were all three baptised.

¶ *There seems to have been two reasons in particular for the attitude of the Jewish Refugee Committee to Christian foster homes. If the parents of the children survived there would be enough barriers to the re-establishing of normal family life without adding that of religion. If the parents did not survive—the Jewish people could not afford to lose the younger generation as well.*

V

¶ *I was not entirely responsible for the boy to whom I gave a home. Financially he was provided for by the church I attended, or rather by some members of it. We paid his school fees between us and bought his clothes. The headmaster took him as a boarder for half fees and he spent his holidays in my home. He was twelve years old when he arrived. I am unmarried and have no children and he became like a son to me and I think he regards me as a mother. He has married a very nice Scottish girl and they have three children. I am often sent for to help, in illness, etc., so I am quite a grandmother! I was an only child and now have no relations alive at all, so it is wonderful for me to have this boy, he has certainly brought great joy into my life.*

¶ *We offered to take a small boy from Germany before war broke out. Owing to his having had some childish illness there was some delay in his arrival and he was three (only just) when he came. As soon as possible he was naturalised and as soon as the law allowed we adopted him. I don't think 'refugee' ever entered his head because from the minute he arrived he was 'our boy'. In fact, as the children grew he was a lovely, sturdy lad and my eldest son was small and thin. Strangers who had been told—by 'friends'?—that we had an adopted son used to think that he must be the one, much to the amusement of the children. He has grown into a tall good-looking young man, he has been well educated and has a very good position and is now happily married. I couldn't wish for a better 'son' and my family are united and happy. He has absorbed our way of doing things because he loved that way, and he and his wife are doing things for their baby as I did for him.*

¶ *We took a girl of sixteen into our home for a time and when she had to leave us she was very upset and so were we, but tried not to show it. We gave her our own front door key so that whatever happened in the future she would always have a home to go to.*

Felicia's Story:

¶ *She came at the age of two and a half with a children's transport, in charge of a sixteen-year-old girl. Four days they travelled; there were no adults with them. She came from Prague. Her mother was a doctor, who was coming to train for a year in England. There was a boy, a little older, but something went wrong with his papers and he didn't get out. The mother didn't get out in time either. We know almost nothing about her background; there is no one who knows now.*

A schoolteacher said she would look after her until the mother came—but couldn't manage her, she was too young. One afternoon two people from the Refugee Committee called and said would we consider her. And I said: 'Well, that's rather extreme.' (We had previously considered taking a sister of a girl whom friends had adopted, she was thirteen years old but didn't get out in time.) But we went to see her, and felt very sorry for her because she was such a tiny little mite. She had been there for one month, during the time four different people had looked after her. And we felt so sorry for the poor mite that we said we would have her. So we just collected her with her bag and things, and took her home. The woman who handed her over knew nothing about us.

When she came we regarded it as a temporary thing, she called us Uncle and Aunt. But she wanted a Mummy and so she called me Aunty Mummy. We spoke no Czech. We had to start with head, eyes, nose, it was a problem to get her to speak English. She wouldn't respond to anything, you couldn't talk to her, play with her, pick her up or nurse her, she just sort of closed up, she was very difficult in the beginning.

After we heard that her parents were dead we adopted her. First we had to get her naturalised, our M.P. did that for us; the Home Secretary said it was very unusual at that age but in the circumstances he would allow it. That was in 1948 when she was twelve.

She was perfectly all right until she was sixteen. Well, we made allowances at times for the difference in nationality which you would expect. We put it down to the fact that she had some idea that she was away from her people. She used to go away into corners by herself, she would never mix with other children. When we took her to tea with former friends of her grandparents she said: 'I don't like them, I don't like the way they talk, they don't talk nice.' She got very fastidious about language for a while, very doubtful of people who didn't speak with perfect English accents. Since then we've found out that she's afraid of everything new. A doctor who knew her then said that she was a normal child with a slightly schizoid personality.

She did quite well scholastically until she was fifteen. She was always slow, very methodical, very thorough, very neat. At fifteen her group sat for O-level G.C.E.; she was a few months too young but she took the papers and the staff said she passed in seven out of eight subjects. The next year, when she was doing A-level work, she took four O-level papers and was just hopeless. That was when she had a nervous breakdown.

The girls told us afterwards that she used to hide in cupboards and corners and cry. The first thing we noticed was that she was never home at the right time, it was always six o'clock or later, and there was never any explanation of where she'd been. But we really knew how ill she was only when we collected her from a holiday by the sea and she kept saying: 'They didn't like me, you see I was too dirty for them. They didn't like my face because my face was dirty.' We took her to the school psychologist and he immediately told us that she was very seriously ill, mentally ill, and he advised us to send her to a hospital in London where they have a special department for young children. Well, we thought, poor Felicia, she's had one separation, we don't want her to have another. So we took her to a local specialist and within six months she was back at school.

But it didn't last. She had another breakdown and since then she has been in and out of hospitals here and in London, with little hope of a permanent cure. The most acute stage of the illness seems to have passed, leaving her with an impaired mentality, very much that of a twelve-year-old girl and a frustrated woman, unable to do the simplest job without much prodding.

The last time she was discharged was in 1959, in May. But since that November she has been living in hospital and only comes home at week-ends. Somebody said to me the other day: 'I don't know how you can do it.' And I said: 'Well, I don't know how I couldn't.' We couldn't let her down. This is Felicia's home and she must come here any time. Nobody will ever feel about her as we do because nobody will ever have known her when she was apparently all right.

But we now think it was a pity that we adopted her. Because she would have remained under the care of the Refugee Committee. What worries us is the future. Who is going to look after her when we are dead? She is no longer a refugee.

INSTITUTIONS

¶ I came as a boy of eight and for the next three years I lived in four different Homes and went to five different schools, until my mother was able to make a home for my brother and me.

¶ I was eleven years old when my parents sent me to England through the Barbican Mission to the Jews, an evangelical society which wanted to convert Jews to Christ's teaching, or rather to their interpretation of it. I was in their care for five and a half years, during which time they fed and clothed me and about forty to fifty other refugee boys. They were altogether miserable, barren, fruitless years.

¶ I am a Roman Catholic and was seventeen years old when I was sent by an aunt who was my sponsor into a convent. After the outbreak of war the nuns refused to keep me, being very anti-German as they were French, and I was sent to a very third-rate school as 'French Mademoiselle' to teach French and almost everything else besides for no pay and so little keep that I was rescued from there half-starved by my aunt after three weeks.

¶ Mr. Burke, having picked me out, had to wait to fetch me as there was an outbreak of scarlet fever in the camp. Of course I looked forward to the wonderful home I was to be taken into, which indeed it was, to begin with. Apparently his mother, a kind, stern, Victorian lady, put up the money while he got a parish from his bishop which had a very large Elizabethan vicarage where he proposed to give a home to several refugee boys. His sister, who was living with the mother on private means, agreed to join him and run the place with a couple of servants. Mr. Burke sent me a card which I still have, describing my future home, with its lovely moat all round the house and the toy boats that could be sailed on it. I spent that summer getting acclimatised to my new surroundings, learning a few more words of English and after a month or so going to the local village school. Being one of the small boys I began to come in for bullying in the Home, which got so bad that Mr. Burke had to send one of the boys back to

Ipswich refugee camp, at which time he took another boy, this time of Jewish faith, back in exchange. (The rest of us were only partly Jews and had been brought up as Christians.) But for me things got much worse. For quite apart from the deepening realisation that my separation from my parents was likely to last a long time because of the war, the intransigent Victorian disciplinary attitude of Mr. Burke (he was an ex-orphanage warden) did not allow him to remain the kind avancular figure I thought he was. Corporal and other types of punishment became the rule of practically every day from about the time I was eleven until I was fourteen. During this time the mother died, and because of death duties much less money was now available. Tempers and discipline got worse, so unbearable that several of us tried to run away. One of the two English boys made it back to his native Sheffield. I did not get very far, but things were a little better after the attempt. Then the little money which I believe Mr. Burke was getting from some authority or other, which was a very small amount, was stopped when the boy reached employable age, and although I continued with my lessons at the Rectory for a while, there was no money at all to educate me and I had to go out to work when I was fifteen; although Mr. Burke never took a penny of my wages. Though in lodgings in the town, I was regularly going home to the Rectory most week-ends; now that I was older relations were much improved and anyway there was nowhere else for me to go. In a more adult light, I saw that my years with them had not been at all what I in my necessity had imagined them to be. Later, it became painfully clear how deluded I had been as a youngster to think that I was ever anything else to them than a refugee boy.

¶ When I arrived in England I was fifteen years old and went with my sister to stay with Mrs. Freeman at Welcome House, her Home for refugee children. This Home was run on family lines, and while there were naturally clashes of personality, it is none the less true and remarkable that we were really—despite all the circumstances—as happy as adolescents are likely to be. This was largely due to Mrs. Freeman's own personality and influence. Originally she had the help of a committee of local do-gooders; with the outbreak of war most of these withdrew. After all, the children were German, and war meant that this was likely to be more than a temporary bit of help. The original Welcome House was closed, Mrs. Freeman moved us into her own home, though the children wrought a good deal of havoc in a beautiful house and garden. Her inspiration was largely religious—she was a Christian and we were only partly Jewish. Where there were no other funds (there usually were not) she made herself entirely responsible for the educational expense as well as the maintenance of the children. Usually there were twelve of us. Six of us were there throughout the war years. As others managed for instance to join their parents in Peru; she refilled the vacant places with children whose original sponsors were abandoning them. When the bombing of London reached its climax she offered my parents a home as well. In the case of myself and my sister her help was forthcoming also for higher education.

¶ *Riversmead, just inside the West Riding, had been empty for some time. It was re-furnished and equipped with new things entirely. The building was rambling and not really suitable for the purpose but was in a wonderful position surrounded by moors, hills and the river below. Two parties of boys arrived (of about thirty each) in June and July 1939, approximately half from Germany and half from Austria. Later, other boys arrived in twos and threes. The committee had been especially asked to take older boys as it had been found more difficult to find private homes for these. Of the staff, about half were themselves refugees. Later, several were interned and replaced with English staff. School was on the premises, with qualified teachers. As the boys' English improved they attended evening classes and later day-schools in nearby towns. Later, friends in Birmingham found jobs in that area for many, but the fact that they were classified as enemy aliens closed many avenues and many had to take employment which would not have been chosen for them in peace time. The younger boys had better opportunities because, by the time they reached school-leaving age, it was possible for them to take up specialised training and higher education.*

II

¶ When I came to this country as a boy of fourteen and wanted to settle down as a human being, I became a sort of museum piece. I was identified with German or Austrian nationality, which I was really wanting to discard—which, according to who was talking at the time, was either good or bad or just curious. Trying to fit into an English school was difficult, because of the strong emphasis on the practical—not only on sport but also on a sense of humour which I could not at first understand.

¶ I came at the age of fourteen and went to Winchester seven months after my arrival, barely a year after leaving a German Gymnasium. I did not enjoy Winchester very much initially, but I think this was only in small part due to the fact that I was still slightly foreign and therefore different from the other boys. I come from a liberal Jewish family and was thus able to accept to some extent the liberal Anglican tone of Winchester. When I was about sixteen or seventeen I began positively to enjoy the life of the school so that I was able to look back with some nostalgia when I left.

¶ I was fifteen years old when I came. My guarantors were the West London Synagogue, who had arranged for me to go to a girls' boarding school in Sussex, mainly to learn the language. I was extremely unhappy there and at the end of the first term asked to be removed. I was not offered a place in another school, but asked what work I would like to do.

¶ I was sixteen years old when I came and went to a domestic science school in Dorset with a friend. On the whole we had a very pleasant year there. . . . But both of us caught lice from the domestic staff, and to our young minds it seemed the worst thing that could happen to us.

¶ I was eleven years old when I came and I must have been a headache to the committee, but at the third attempt they placed me with the headmistress of a girls' boarding school and there I was quite happy—although she had a good old-fashioned Victorian attitude that one must always be grateful. Whenever I was in trouble and this was pretty frequently, I was always reminded of how much I owed to the headmistress who had given me a home and a place which another child would have filled more profitably. . . . And so although I barely understood the word refugee I was only too fully aware of being different from the other girls.

¶ I was ten years old when I came and was sent to a boarding school which catered largely for girls whose parents were in India. On my arrival I was introduced to a smelly pekingese called Toto and told that I would have the privilege of looking after him. The

3*

idea was probably that it was good for my soul to do something towards my keep; who was paying my fees never bothered me and I don't think I was deliberately vague about this: I was just naïve about money matters at that time. There may have been kindliness in the idea that this way I would have something to love, but Toto became the bane of my life. I felt like a charity child because I had to look after him. I knew nothing about dogs and was forever doing the wrong thing. I loathed him but hugged him when I was miserable. My first months were unhappy because I became self-conscious and lost confidence in myself. The first general remark on my report was 'Is a little serious for her age.' I was quickly promoted to a higher class but was told that although I was doing well academically—from then on I always came top in English—I was selfish because I did not take enough interest in what went on around me. My shyness must have had something to do with being a refugee for until I came to England I was open, cheerful, good at repartee with my elders and this in spite of being much more aware of what was going on at home and in Germany in general than my mother realised. The staff were very kind to me and the pupils accepted me. There were, however, certain occasions which were agony. One of these was being weighed and measured each term. For some reason I did not grow at all for about a year. This was always commented on in a jocular way by Toto's owner: 'Did Mr. Hitler put a weight on your head?' I remember thinking melodramatically how I used to read adventure stories at home and, reflecting on my relatively ordinary existence, wish something would happen to me, and now when things had happened my dearest wish was to be just like everybody else. I used to envy the other girls the luxury of homesickness for I had no home to be sick for. I used to miss my mother a great deal, while her extremely affectionate letters and the odd bar of chocolate embarrassed me. She came to see me once and was not allowed to stay because she was an enemy alien and this was a protected area. I went to the police station with her where she appealed to the humanity of the man in charge and said that she would even spend a night in a cell. I was relieved when she left and missed her dreadfully. My twin brother was allowed to visit me occasionally on Sunday afternoons or I would go to his 'family' where the relief of being in a normal home atmosphere was enormous although I felt responsible for his being naughty. After the school was evacuated my mother was offered the post of matron; of course she accepted to be with me. Her physical endurance was severely taxed—she had had sciatica very badly in Germany, and she always suffered from chilblains; she was treated rudely and I hated her being there. I hated, too, her rather ostentatious affection for me, and the feeling of exclusion when the other girls apologised to me for giving her a nickname like the rest of the staff. She had a kimono-type dressing gown and they called her the Chinese monstrosity. They liked her and I knew they did, but I should have preferred her to have been elsewhere. I was unreasonably sensitive about her accent too. Occasionally I was invited to spend part of the holidays at my 'guardian's' house. I used to feel everybody was kind but rather patronising: handed-down clothes and offers to put my Teutonic plaits up round my head. I also knew that my sister had stayed there once but, when some friends were expected, she was given five shillings to take herself off to the pictures. (I genuinely like the family; they are just lacking in imagination sometimes and perhaps, had they had more tact and less efficiency, they would not have got us out of Germany in time.) Once we discussed emigration at their dinner table and my 'guardian' said what a splendid thing it might be for my brother and me to go to Australia: after all, we had no roots. I felt very shocked and aggrieved: I had been trying so hard to put down roots; when my mother spoke to me in German, I always replied in English; there was no Jewish community with which I had contact nor did I meet fellow-refugees; I was going to marry an Englishman and call my children John and Elisabeth and be as English as anything.

¶ I was ten years old when I came and after a foster home my sister and I were sent to Stoatley Rough School in Surrey, where we stayed throughout the war, both matriculating there. It was founded in the early thirties for refugees by Dr. Hilde Lion. It was attended by a few English children also, but they were a minority. Stoatley Rough was more than a boarding school, it was a real home for most of the seventy odd children whose parents were either in the States, having emigrated separately, or, in many cases, the children were orphans, though we did not know it yet.

¶ *The two girls were sent to England by their father when they were eleven and twelve years old, in the winter of 1938-39; he had made an arrangement with an English friend of his to act as their guardian. They were to be at an independent boarding school; he had plenty of money and there was no question of their being a liability to anyone. However, when war broke out it became impossible for him to send any more money and the following winter their English guardian dropped dead, having, naturally enough, made no mention of the girls in her will. So there they were, completely cut off from home and financial aid, in a very expensive school and with no one whatever to look after them and their interests in any way. In September 1939 I had become headmistress of the school—a rather strange appointment as I was then a young girl in my twenties—and I found the girls there, destitute and friendless. The Governors of the school felt that they could not stay there indefinitely without paying and with nobody to be responsible for them in the holidays and to act as a parent. I, young, idealistic and compassionate, felt they could not possibly be turned out and sent to an orphanage; they were just beginning to feel at home and the staff and the girls there represented the only 'family' they could now be said to have got. After endless arguments and discussions (complicated by the fact that I was engaged to be married and had my future husband, as well as the School Governors to convince) I was allowed to adopt the children by means of a special wartime adoption order. It was a temporary measure and remained in force only until (if ever) the children could be restored to their real parents. The Governors allowed the girls to stay in the school without paying as long as I acted as their mother (which I was much too young, in fact, to be) and arranged for their holidays etc. They were certainly most unattractive children, poor little things, and it was very hard to love them. They were very plain, quarrelled unceasingly and found it very difficult to become integrated into the community. Margaret was determined from the very first to become English; she pretended to have forgotten the German language, as soon as she had learned English, and resolutely refused ever to speak a word of German or to help with translating it or anything like that. She clamoured to be baptised and confirmed into the Church of England for this reason alone, I am sure. She ceased to be called 'Grete' by which name she was always known at school and insisted on her full name of Margaret, which is also an English name. She made every conceivable effort to disguise her markedly foreign appearance. As soon as it was legally possible she became a naturalised British subject, and she soon succeeded in her determination to find a British husband and produce some English children! Anne showed none of this repudiation of her own nationality; she did eventually become naturalised, but not in any frantic hurry and not without much thought. Gradually the children calmed down; they were no longer 'the two Austrians' to be pointed out to visitors as if they were a pair of wild animals. They were accepted as two ordinary members of the school, no more or less interesting than any others, and as the community forgot their differences, so these differences disappeared.*

Bunce Court:

¶ *Anna Essinger started Bunce Court in Kent in 1933, with 75 children between the ages of six and sixteen from her school in Germany. In 1938–39 she took about a hundred of those who came with the children's transports. The first ten she brought from Dovercourt, chosen on the basis of her private feelings; she thought they would fit in and she would like them and she could give them something. The oldest we got were thirteen. Anna wanted young ones she would have for some time. One boy's sister was fourteen and she was too old to come. But some who came were only three because they had an older brother or sister.*

Sometimes nobody paid for them, sometimes English people did. In the beginning everybody had 200 Marks, and money could still be sent from Germany. After that stopped we got money through the committee, and from America or Africa or wherever relations lived. One night we had no money any more—that was at the beginning of the war. Anna went to London, and we all waited and waited and kept the children singing so that they would not notice that there was no supper.

She often went to London to raise funds, she went to the committee and wherever she was invited to speak about the school. Once somebody asked her to come to tea, to meet Iris Origo; she didn't want to go, she said: 'I never go to tea, my time is too precious.' The friend said: 'I beg you to come, it will help the school,' and we all said: 'Go, go, go.' Iris Origo is English, married to an Italian Count. She said: 'How can I help you?' And Anna said there were many ways, to invite a child for the holidays or to pay his school fees and keep for a year, or we had a building fund—just money, we always needed money. And she said: 'I think I'll pay school fees for ten children.' That meant that ten children could be brought out of Germany because there was a guarantor for them. She said: 'Pick ten children to bring out and I will pay for them. Pick small children, so they will be with you a long time.' And then she gave us a thousand pounds for the building fund.

To prepare the children for life in England, as they were so cut off in the country, Anna always tried to find families who would take them for holidays, so that they would see English life and only hear and speak English. She did not choose only Jewish families, but who-ever was humanly nice and invited children. Quaker families invited many. When people asked: 'What can we do for the school?' Anna always said: 'If you like and have children of your own you can in-vite a child for holidays', and when it worked the first time the people invited them again, and it became an institution that they always went there. Even before the war she already had an English family for every child.

When the children came they were very disturbed and very restless and very unhappy, because they had lost their homes and their parents; first they had their loss and then they settled here and took it for granted and enjoyed their daily life. And only when they left school and had to go out on their own, then it came again, the realisa-tion that they were alone in the world and had no one. They settled here or in another school, where they lived and loved and were loved, and afterwards they were again lost, and had again unsettled ex-periences. And then, only then, they settled and became English.

Whittingehame House:
¶　*This Farm School was part of the English Youth Aliyah Move-ment, which provided training for hundreds of boys and girls waiting to migrate to Palestine. I became matron there when the school opened on 15th February 1939.*

The local Scottish Committee of School Governors devoted an enormous amount of time and effort to the school and they were generous and helpful even if they did not understand the children's point of view. There was, for instance, the question of pooling all the pocket money decided on in one of the school meetings. That smacked too much of communism to please Edinburgh business men. Or of less importance—I ordered cake for the Sabbath breakfast. 'Cake for breakfast?' It seemed awful to the Edinburgh people (including the baker). But it came punctually every Friday.

Less understanding was shown by the London Committee. I hardly believed my eyes when I unpacked some sample clothes for the chil-

dren: they all were khaki coloured. So I sat down and wrote in my best—not very good—English that design and quality of the garments were excellent and very acceptable but that I could not ask continental children to wear brown uniforms, after their experiences with the Brownshirts from whom they had just escaped. Navy blue was decided upon instead.

There were numerous visitors to the school. The children hated to be kept waiting for them and to be talked down to. They resented being told to be grateful for the refuge they had found. Most of them cold-shouldered the journalists who beleaguered the grounds in the first few weeks out for sensational stories. What should have been an attentive, reverent audience at pious stories and exhortations was often a giggling crowd—on the other hand nobody laughed at one woman's valiant attempt to speak to them in their own language.

For some of the English teachers these foreign children were as strange as beings from another world; they had never seen such a lack of conformity, which resulted from the fact that they not only came from very varied social backgrounds and every part of Middle Europe but had also not undergone the levelling training of an English school.

The attempt of one headmaster to run Whittingehame as a Jewish Eton was not appreciated by the children; their ideal was a Kibbutz, not an English public school. But the same headmaster was intelligent and great-hearted enough to participate in the pervading ideological spirit, even as far as learning and performing a large part in a Hebrew play.

There was laziness and indifference amongst the children, especially in the first year of their stay, most probably aggravated by long times spent waiting in reception camps with hardly any work or tuition or leadership. So it was not a rare sight to see a group of boys playing football when they should have been in class learning English or arithmetic—there was much less absenteeism from practical work.

Lord Balfour's house had to withstand considerable wear and tear; during a short stay in the sickroom one boy dismantled the electrical fittings so thoroughly that not even the electrician could put them together again. The problems proper seem not to have originated in the school but might have become severer through the shock of emigration: the bedwetting boys were probably afflicted before they came. Insecurity became manifest in overbearing as well as cringing attitudes—the latter much more among the girls.

*Later work improved, even in school, when the youngsters realised
how much teaching they had missed by being excluded from their
German schools at the age of twelve or thirteen. The same girls who
at first followed only reluctantly, if at all, expert advice when doing
domestic chores, were now eager to learn the correct way of doing
things; standards of gracious middle-class living deliberately sup-
pressed and rejected at the beginning came to the surface when they
hankered for the jobs in the headmaster's flat, where a less institu-
tional way of life prevailed.*

*That boys and girls were on the right road to a healthy develop-
ment of their personalities was borne out by the test put upon the
school by outside events; in June 1940 a great number of boys were
interned as 'enemy aliens', and the girls took over heavy work and
greater responsibilities.*

*When the school was closed about two years later—it had never
been intended as a permanent establishment—the boys began to earn
their living as agricultural labourers and the girls as domestic
servants.*

III

¶ I was eleven years old when I came and was sent to a Jewish
hostel for boys in Leeds; my older brother was also sent to a
hostel but in another town. At first there were about eighty boys,
but the number slowly decreased as boys left for various reasons.
Although I am very grateful to the people who paid money for
the hostel and its upkeep, whose existence no doubt saved my
life, I do not consider the hostel to have been a happy or pleasant
place. At the beginning it was all right but later it got worse
mainly through a change in the management. But of course children and young men were there from different countries and different types of homes and it would have been a miracle had we all
blended together in harmony. At fourteen years we had to leave
school and find some work. We had to give up nearly all our
wages. But we also had some good times there, such as playing
football, being taken to the cinema, a pantomime at Christmas,
etc.

¶ After a brief stay in a foster home I was sent at the age of fourteen to a hostel for refugee girls. This was beautifully furnished
and kept and I remember thinking even then that a few luxuries
less would have enabled a few more children to be taken in. We

had dancing lessons and were sometimes invited to tea or lunch to the very luxurious homes of the committee ladies. My stay there was only temporary. I was 'filling in' for another girl who had not yet arrived. So after a few weeks I was sent to stay with a very nice family over Passover. I am still in touch with these people—one daughter was about my age and we are still friends. However, I could not stay there and was then sent to another family. All this time I had not been to school or learned anything. I spent my time writing dozens of letters to my family and friends —now all over the world. What saved me in those days were the free public libraries, where I was able to get books in German and so read the classics and I also tried to teach myself English by reading all I could with the help of dictionaries. Eventually I was sent to another hostel, a lovely house with a big garden right down to the sea. We were about eighteen girls, mostly from Germany. I was apprenticed to a hairdresser, not because I was particularly interested in becoming a hairdresser, but it seemed better than the other offers of domestic work etc. I earned 2s. 6d. a week and lived at the hostel.

¶ After a few months at Dovercourt some of us, all boys of about sixteen, were placed in a hostel in Oxford; most of us then attended the School of Technology, Art and Commerce. In June 1940 the entire hostel was interned as enemy aliens.

¶ When I left my foster home I was sent to a hostel in London. There were about thirty or forty boys, most of whom I had known at Dovercourt. The hostel was situated in a large house but not large enough for such a crowd. In the two dormitories the beds were no more than two feet apart. There was a good deal of grumbling about conditions and the discipline. Every Friday was settling night. Full board and lodgings had been fixed at 25s. per week and whoever earned more than that could do as he liked with the balance. There were only two or three boys who did. The rest of us handed our total earnings over and were then given our bus fares to get to work for the following week and 2s. pocket money. The hostel itself was subsidised partly by the local refugee committee and partly by the Children's Movement. Two shillings did not go far even then. It could not all be spent on pleasure, one had to buy soap, razor blades, toothpaste and such necessities. Still, there were ways of supplementing one's pocket money. By getting off the bus a fare stage earlier and walking the rest I

saved a shilling a week and soon I could count on two regular tips
of 6d. each. In this way I managed to buy the odd shirt or to have
my suit cleaned.

¶   I spent the war years in a refugee hostel in Glasgow. This
hostel was in many respects exceptional, as the Jewish community who supported it enabled anyone who was able to continue
his education. In fact it was the only hostel where a large number
of boys were able to go on to university. The examination results
did us great credit. For anyone not to finish with a first class
degree was a rare exception. But owing to the plight of my
parents, who had come to England just before the war, I decided
to go to work immediately; I was fourteen years old. I took an
apprenticeship in tailoring and eventually entered the wholesale
mantle trade. I spent most of my evenings at night school both at
the Glasgow School of Art and at the Technical College. I was
fortunate that the atmosphere of the hostel was stimulating to
learning and reading, and those of us who were working were
greatly helped by the students. I became a shop steward and
member of my union executive by the time I was eighteen.

¶   I came at the age of ten and was sent to a refugee hostel for
twenty-four girls. I have seen the two matrons since those days
and realise that they have no idea of how the life there affected
many of us. A local committee provided the money and I think
on a physical level we were generously catered for and well looked
after. I feel, however, that mentally many of us suffered greatly in
that atmosphere for such a long period during our adolescence.
This was in part due to war circumstances, to the desperate homesickness we experienced, but also because the people who looked
after us were not really suited to their task. Neither of them had
any experience of dealing with young girls, and both were in the
same unhappy position as we were, having left members of their
families behind. Consequently the atmosphere in the hostel was
more often than not very unhappy. We had absurd rules; sometimes we were not allowed to speak German, which was ludicrous
as most of us had not yet acquired enough English to fill the need.
We were constantly told to be silent, and had whole periods of the
day when we were not allowed to talk, and at times were forbidden to laugh. More serious was the distinction made between
different nationalities, and the hypocrisy over religious matters.
The matrons were Austrians and made it clear that they preferred

the Austrians and Czechs; though this may not have been as seriously intended as we then felt it to be. As we were largely supported by money collected from orthodox Jews, the hostel was supposed to be run on fairly orthodox lines, and most of us realised that this was done insincerely. We were constantly reminded that we had to be grateful, and whenever visitors came we had to appear in a body and group ourselves together and smile. This we called *die Affenschau*. Now I realise and appreciate that my life was in fact saved; at the time I bitterly resented the hostel and longed to be with my parents no matter where they were. Fortunately we had one contact with normal life—school. We were pupils in an ordinary, friendly English school, with kind, understanding teachers. Conditions were poor, the school was overcrowded with evacuees, the teachers were overworked, the syllabus old-fashioned, and we loved it. We were different from the others but accepted by them. Only very rarely did we have to face hostility because we were officially German. For me the difficulties and unhappiness of hostel life resolved themselves by my being expelled. I was seventeen and still attending school— my school having persuaded me to embark on a 6th-form course. This was against hostel policy, we were to leave school at fourteen and take up jobs. An exception had been made for me, and was later regretted. I was told either to leave the school or the hostel. This was extremely difficult, as I had no other home. Fortunately the head of my school resolved this problem by letting me live with her, thus enabling me to finish my school career. From then on life became much easier and happier, in spite of the ever-present feeling of debts to others and a basic insecurity.

¶ At the beginning of the war, when I was fifteen, I was sent to a girls' hostel, where I soon learned that all they cared about was that we should have a roof over our heads and not actually go hungry. We were constantly reminded by our ladies from the committee that we depended on charity and since most of the money was donated in the U.S.A. little of the funds were arriving in this country. We only received coppers for pocket money; when we requested fare money or stamps we were told: 'If people want to keep in touch with you they have to pay for this themselves.' If one decided to go for a long walk this was interpreted as using the committee's money because one was wearing out the soles of one's shoes. They were never tired of reminding us that we were lucky to be in this country—and so we were—but few attempts were made to make our lives a little happier. Our hostel matron, however, tried everything in her power to take our parents' place and to guide our thinking and behaviour into right and decent channels. It is with great gratitude that I remember her and her influence on my life.

¶ When I was fifteen years old I left my foster home and stayed for six months in a badly run and almost completely unorganised hostel. Most of the boys were a lot older than I and I was badly bullied by everyone. Almost every week I pleaded with the authorities at Bloomsbury House to change my lodgings. 'You must be grateful for what you have,' I was told. 'You're lucky to be here,' was another staple remark. I obtained work at a printer's and received 25s. a week. One pound of this had to be given up towards my keep. But I could make use of the free clothing store at Bloomsbury House every six months, I was told, and providing I behaved I would receive a cinema voucher every week. Oh, how miserable I was. How lonely I felt.

¶ I was fortunate to be sent to Ramsgate Hostel, a place with a family atmosphere, one that was designed to minimise any problems of homelessness and homesickness. It housed about fifteen teen-age boys from Germany and Austria. There were the usual petty rivalries and fights among the boys, as well as a minor division along nationality lines. Apart from eating well and enjoying our environment by taking long walks, we did little but study English, read, write letters, listen to the radio, and—last but definitely not least—clean the house. It was in the nature of things that most refugee boys were barred from continuing their schooling, and I recall only one or two boys being apprenticed with a view to learning a trade. After the beginning of war we were transferred to the Chiltern Emigrants Training Colony at Benson, near Reading, which was operated by the Christian Service Union for mentally retarded British boys. We took our meals (and very bad ones they were) in a common dining hall and occasionally played soccer and cricket with the British boys, but otherwise had little contact with them; actually, they seemed harmless and pleasant enough. About sixty of us refugee boys were housed in three rather primitive, heatless barracks; some worked in pig-sties and cow-sheds, others trimmed hedges and built fences or roads. I was put in a sort of unskilled labour battalion which worked in a gravel pit. The contrast between Ramsgate and Benson could hardly have been greater. The warmth and security of family-style life was replaced by the impersonal coldness of army-style living, and at sixteen I was not ready for this.

EARLY SCHOOLDAYS AND INTERNMENT

I

¶ At Dovercourt, all of us had the chance to learn some English. Some did and some didn't and it did not seem to depend on age or intelligence.

¶ I fought against the need to learn English for years—I think because the German language was all that was left to me of my childhood and I did not want to give it up.

¶ Because I knew no English I was put with the Infants when I started school and this confirmed the inferiority I had felt in Germany as a Jew—here I was inferior because I was a foreigner.

¶ We had learned sufficient English after a few weeks to begin school, but of course it was a very broken English, and I can remember my unhappiness at being laughed at by the other children because of our accents and incorrect way of speaking.

¶ I appeared to learn English fairly quickly. This was probably due to necessity rather than skill as I knew absolutely no one who could understand German and I became desperate to make myself understood.

¶ We were told that we must learn English before going to school. As we could not do this while we played only with each other, we started school after all and immediately picked up English very easily.

¶ We started school almost immediately and I remember well my first day. My knowledge of English at that time was limited to about ten words, and sign language proved very useful. The children were extremely kind and helpful to us and I made several friends. During that time, my desire for reading matter became an obsession but there was no German literature available. In desperation I began to struggle with English books and, after a couple of months, was able to read them. This helped me tremendously with my language problem and in no time at all I was bi-lingual.

¶ I remember using phrases not knowing the actual meaning of them, but being sure of the desired effect. After some months I had almost overnight given up translating from one language into the other and of course from that moment on things improved greatly.

¶ The first six months at school were spent in learning English and attempts to master coinage, measurements, weights and such matters. The language I conquered with fair rapidity and reasonable success, though the other matter eluded my complete mastery then as now.

¶ I recall one particular occasion at school when I was the only member of my class able to spell the word 'beautiful' correctly; the teacher said that she thought it remarkable that the only pupil to spell the word correctly was a foreigner.

¶ There were several refugee children and our foster parents insisted that we should try to speak English among ourselves. They were both very kind but very severe. If we spoke German while we were at the table, we had to leave our meal and go straight up to bed. This was the worst punishment given to us for any misdemeanour. Looking back on this now, I feel grateful for their wisdom. In less than six months I not only understood simple conversation, but was able to read newspapers and write. After two years my cousin was top of the class in English and I was fourth. The teachers were proud of us and we would always be given as an example to the rest of the class.

¶ I certainly learned English much more quickly than my parents; not only because of my youthful brain but because I heard English all day at school while they tended to gather round them their German-speaking friends. Within six months I spoke English almost fluently. Confirmation of this milestone in my life came with my school report at the end of my second term: English—No. in class 30—Position 1st. It was simply that I had had the incentive and the curiosity and the extra consciousness of English grammar with which to meet the challenge of learning a new language.

¶ I very soon spoke perfect English—without accent, although of course I forgot my German in the process.

¶ After a year I had learned enough English to pass the entrance examination to the Grammar School. From then on, for the next three or four years, I felt, and tried to become, as English as I was ever likely to be. I spoke no German. I renounced my background; I was ashamed of it. I wanted to forget everything. If I was asked where I came from it was tantamount to being accused of a crime. To be reminded that I was Austrian, or worse still, Jewish, and a refugee child, was an insult. But one day I met an elderly man, like myself a refugee from Vienna. I met him at a friend's house. We spoke, naturally enough, in German; he remembered details and people I had long succeeded in forgetting. And it all came back. I remembered who I was. I was never likely to forget it again.

II

¶ *Concerning the evacuation of schoolchildren, I have everywhere the assurance that the family will treat the child as their own, and unless there is interference from the police or the military I believe that all our alien children will be as safe as our own, which is as far as we can go in planning. The goodness of guardians and friends is everywhere most heartening, as is the gratitude of the children.*
—*From the Children's Report of a Local Refugee Committee.*

¶ The declaration of war shattered my hard-won sense of security. The final blow was the news that we were on the move again. We'd hardly been a year at our present address and now we were to be evacuated. My feelings in the car as it drove out of London and into the country lanes were exactly the same, I remember, as on the train out of Germany: a sort of frustrated anger at being forced to move and bewildered despair at not knowing quite why we were moving.

¶ Hardly had we settled down to our new life when war broke out and we were evacuated like all the other schoolchildren. For my brother and me it was our third home and our third school in the space of twelve months.

¶ The hostel had to close down as we were all officially enemy aliens, and we were on the coast in a protected area. All the girls were sent to another hostel but as I was still under sixteen I was allowed to stay. I went to live with the people for whom I was working.

¶ My foster parents decided to evacuate themselves to the country. We were to leave in the evening and at midday they found out that the place of their choice was a protected area where

I would not be allowed to live. What was to be done with me? I had one friend who had just come to London and lived with her parents in one large room. My case was packed in no time and within an hour I was deposited on their doorstep.

¶ *I went to see the boys who had been evacuated; they looked rather dubious, I think they felt that they had been forsaken: added to which there was an aura of fear. They had once again been plunged into what seemed to them a hostile environment. None of them had been in England for more than a year, and a few of them had only just arrived.*

III

¶ To be told that the country of my birth was the declared enemy of the country of my adoption was hardly conducive to the settling-down process. Not that my loyalties were divided: I was definitely for England and against Germany. I learned very quickly to omit any reference to my nationality when being introduced to people, and I adopted the same attitude to my religion. At this time I wanted above all to be 'accepted' and that meant pretending to be as average and English as possible.

¶ After the war started I remember some building workers calling 'Jerries' after us—none of us understood what it meant, of course.

¶ At first it was very hard having to learn English at school, over and over again being called a refugee, spy etc. I often wept a lot. After a time I got so used to it, it did not bother me any more.

¶ By the time I started school in the first spring of the war I was already accomplished at concealing my origin. But it was difficult to keep up the pretence amongst my fellow schoolboys. They laughed at the long shiny raincoat I was wearing. I hadn't realised until then that a lot of my clothes were different from theirs. They laughed at my attempts to speak English (I'd made very little progress with the language as everyone at home spoke German). They surrounded me in the playground and forced me to say something in German, and then ran giggling to their friends to try and repeat what I'd said. Inside the classroom I felt even more of an outcast. I was never much good at arithmetic but to try to follow subtraction sums in foreign money explained in a foreign

language was more than I could bear. Often I arrived back home
in tears.

¶   I didn't want to be known as a foreigner, having by that time
learned something of the common English attitude to foreigners
and I especially resented being called a German. 'Austrian' wasn't
too bad, for after all Austria had herself been a victim of Nazism.
I was furious when I was nicknamed 'Girder' at school and
wished I hadn't such a silly name as Gerda and a surname which
I had always to spell out to people.

¶   I lied about my birth but I realised that I was different, and
always coming top of the class did not help.

¶   I used to feel terribly embarrassed when people asked me to
'say something in German' and always refused to oblige.

¶   During the war, I hated to have to tell anyone that I was born
in Germany and when people talked about the Germans and how
they hated them, I took it as personal and felt awful. Although I
had more reason than most to hate them.

¶   The fact that I had a half-brother who was eleven years older
than I and whom I hardly knew, and who to top it all was in the
Luftwaffe, was a great trial to me. I remember I tore up all photos
I happened to have of him and never breathed a word to a soul
that he existed. To this day I say that I am an only child and to all
intents and purposes this is indeed so. Imagine what hell I would
have had to live with if the children at school, who mostly had
brothers or fathers in the war, had found out that I had a brother
in the Luftwaffe!

¶   Most of the teachers were very kind to us and understanding.
Our history master, however, was just plain anti-German and
even though it must have been clear to him that as Jews we had
certainly no sympathy for the German cause, he would take great
delight in making remarks which were most unkind. One day he
told me that the British soldiers were the best in the world and
added: 'You people did not think we had it in us.' I don't think
he had anything against us boys, but he just did not appreciate
our position.

¶   I just went on at school—trying not to be noticed. Occasionally by some obscure and innocently intended action one
would be picked out. I remember an incident when we all
went into a room which was rather cold, and I shivered. The
teacher with us said in her wonderfully piercing upper-class

voice: 'People in England don't shiver when they come into a cold room, there isn't enough coal because we're fighting the *Germans*.'

¶ My father joined the Pioneer Corps as soon as this was possible. So I was always pointed out as the little German girl whose Daddy was fighting in the British Army.

¶ The owners of a small private school decided that their particular charity would be to give an education to a refugee child, and that child was I. They not only remitted my fees but bought all my uniforms, and everyone knew that I was somehow on a level with the boy whose mother did some of the cleaning. I was rather a nine days' wonder—most of the children had expected a little black girl—and they all called me 'Leeley'—whether they thought that this was better or more exotic than just Lilly I do not know.

¶ I was very unhappy at all the schools I went to, four in all, though I did settle down better at the last one. I suppose I was older and maybe had become resigned and more ready to accept things.

IV

¶ If the British at first underestimated the might of the Germans, I on the other hand tended to overestimate their power, having so recently escaped. . . .

¶ The warden of our hostel saw me laughing and asked: 'What have you got to laugh about? You have been classified as an enemy alien.'

¶ I was interned as an enemy alien in 1940, a thing which was a great shock to me as, naturally, there was nothing 'enemy' about my feelings for this country, and it was a pretty awful moment for me when I, a girl of seventeen, was fetched by two (kind) policemen and shipped off to an 'unknown' destination. Actually I was quite comfortable on the Isle of Man.

¶ My brother was interned on the Isle of Man. I was exempted from internment, after appearing before a tribunal on my 16th birthday. In 1942 my brother was released and started work on a farm.

¶ In June 1940 the entire hostel at Oxford was interned as enemy aliens. After a few days at a camp near Paignton and several weeks in a tented camp at Press Heath, Wilts., I finished up at Onchan, Isle of Man, where I stayed until my release in June 1941, when I joined the Pioneer Corps.

¶ In October 1940 I joined my mother on the Isle of Man where we stayed until 1942, when we were released, as my brother had, in the meantime, joined the army. Life was pleasant on the Isle of Man and I have wonderful memories of the 'camp'. In fact, we were better off than most people in London.

¶ At the beginning of the war, in the autumn of 1939, I had, like all aliens, to appear before a tribunal to be classified into one of three categories—one meant immediate internment, the intermediate one meant restrictions such as curfew and a five mile travel limit; I was put into the last, 'Refugee from Nazi Oppression', which apart from general restrictions, such as prohibition to drive and use a camera, meant exemption from internment.

In May 1940, however, during the panic over the fall of France and the possibility of a German invasion these categories were abandoned and all male aliens were interned and many deported to Canada and Australia.

One day in June two policemen arrived at my home searching the house 'for bombs' (sic!)—carrying off an extraordinary mixture of papers, such as letters from my parents, books, especially things written in German—and arresting me. I was allowed to pack one suitcase and take one coat.

In the police car we picked up another 'German'—he had lived in an English village since the First World War, had never bothered or had been too poor to become naturalised, but had almost forgotten his German origin!

At an army camp near Corsham we were handed into the custody of the military with several other internees. We were escorted to the station and taken to Salisbury where we spent the night in the police cells. On the way to Salisbury the sergeant in charge seemed to understand our harmlessness and treated us in a very friendly fashion; he even looked the other way when we each posted a card telling our people of our well-being and hoping the date stamp would be legible and tell them where we were at that point! The night was uncomfortable: we were three to a cell and I remember sleeping on a sort of board.

Next morning we were taken to a train—a whole transport of internees. It was difficult to discover where we were going: the large station names had been removed everywhere; no one told us anything; rumours of air-raids and impending invasion were rife; we were allowed no newspaper. We found ourselves arriving at Seaton in South Devon and were taken to a camp, once a holiday camp with chalets, dance-halls, swimming pools, etc. But the atmosphere was not pleasant now: the whole camp was surrounded with barbed wire, electric fences, armed guards, screened with canvas and dotted with look-out towers. We were herded in; the officers had their revolvers drawn. Whenever the sirens went— which seemed to happen frequently—they drove us, blowing their whistles, into the chalets.

However we did not stay long at Seaton—a day or two—and we were taken off on another long train journey. This took all day; we were often left waiting in sidings. It seemed obvious that we were going north, however. To Liverpool perhaps, to be deported overseas? The soldiers and officers did not attempt to scotch rumours. In the evening we disembarked at Bury, Lancashire, which at any rate in 1940 struck me as the dreariest, dirtiest spot on earth—truly hopeless. Our 'camp' was even worse.

It was a disused cotton mill, surrounded by the usual assortment of wire, guards and towers. It was empty; long halls supported on cast-iron pillars; there was oil and dirt everywhere; and there were our 'beds'—straw palliasses, meagre ones, and blankets, laid out in rows along the pillars. When we arrived our suitcases were searched thoroughly—this had already happened in Seaton, but here they were more thorough. Everything was emptied on to the floor; a few essentials were returned to us; the rest was heaped in two piles, one for officers and one for men; they seemed especially keen on toilet articles and stationery. This was a symptom of that time, but was not legal: a year later the commandant of that camp was sentenced to a term of imprisonment for these thefts.

Altogether conditions were primitive; the latrines were of the simplest Army 'field' type, inadequate and unhygienic for our numbers; we were crowded, we were allowed no newspapers; there was nothing to do apart from keeping a minimum standard of cleanliness—and talking. The most serious argument was whether to accept our lot patiently and co-operate with the military as our contribution to the 'war effort'. But many of us felt this was absurd: we were all 'Refugees from Nazi Oppression'; we all feared a Nazi invasion; and yet we were being treated like criminals; even if we could not be free surely we could be treated more humanely? Our fortnightly twenty-four lines of censored communication—on shiny prison paper—with the outside world had brought no replies yet. Even so gradually news began to seep through, news of people concerned about our lot.

One or two people needed dental treatment and were taken to a dentist in the town under escort. They managed to bring back odd pages of newspapers from the waiting room. These quickly circulated throughout the camp. One was a page from the *News Chronicle* containing readers' letters, and there was a letter from my foster mother, protesting strongly against the treatment of internees. Not only that—she quoted a piece from a letter of mine: I had chanced telling her about the real conditions, having nothing more to lose; if the censor thought this unfit for human consumption then the blue lines would tell a strong tale! Had the censor himself been shocked by what he read and did he want the outside world to know? Anyway this newspaper page was like a miracle to us all and we were tremendously comforted.

Then came another piece of news proving that humanity and democracy in England were still alive. The commandant had to communicate to us the fact that a commission of Quakers was visiting the internment camps and was going to come to Bury and would want to hear our comments on conditions; they had obtained permission to do this from the Home Office and War Office! I remember stormy meetings in which most of us insisted that our representatives told them all and showed them all—the crowded dirty 'dormitories' and the latrines included.

After this things slowly began to change. A few weeks later we were moved from our grim mill. Once again we boarded trains, this time to Liverpool and then to the Isle of Man. It was a nightmare journey, incredibly slow and dreary in that worst period of the war. We crossed the Irish Sea during the night; raids and mines were obviously the great danger; but even amongst all this 'they' were still making sure we didn't escape: we were allowed neither on the top decks, nor in the more comfortable quarters of the old ship; we could not see out, for the sides were covered with canvas.

¶ At Ramsey, all the hotels and boarding houses were geographically separate from the town proper, just the other side of the tiny harbour. The whole section had simply been surrounded by a double fence of barbed wire and, hey presto, an internment camp had been created. If one ignored the barbed wire, the group of buildings was very prettily situated, in front the beach and the sea, at the back an ornamental lake and gardens and beyond the hills. But one could not ignore the barbed wire, we were quite literally fenced in. We had lost our liberty, but not, paradoxically, our freedom.

Those first few days were the most depressing of my life. It was my first—and so far only—experience of being imprisoned. For the first time I became fully conscious of how utterly alone I was in the world. The few friends I had made were either in the same position or could not help me anyway. This was the only time when I strongly felt that emotion which is usually called 'home-sickness', but the emotion turned sour since there was no home for which to be sickening.

I had no idea what had happened to my father since the fall of France, my mother interned in darkest Hungary and I cooped up in this place, which, should a German invasion be successful, would have become a concentration camp. I felt very sorry for myself and in this mood volunteered to be sent to Canada or Australia. Fortunately, as a result of protests in the press and in Parliament, these transports were stopped and I remained on the Isle of Man.

I soon got over this bout of self-pity. I was nothing if not good at adapting myself to new circumstances and I was only seventeen. Life at Ramsey settled down to a tolerable routine, which was far from dull. Discomforts there were, to be sure. There wasn't a stick of furniture in any of the houses. We slept on mattresses on the floor, there was of course no bed linen, the windows were painted black, there were no mirrors anywhere and one learned to comb ones hair and shave without them.

The guards were friendly and since no escape attempts were made, their duties were not onerous. Apart from the daily roll-call, we were left entirely to our own devices. These were in some ways quite remarkable. The number of professional men, artists and intellectuals among the inmates was disproportionate and soon made itself felt. For me this became a time of intellectual awakening or rather re-awakening. Since leaving home I had been so busy digesting new impressions and learning English that my mind was fully occupied. The enforced idleness of camp life brought home to me my interrupted education and my ignorance. It was a gradual process, helped perhaps by my frequenting the company of older men in search of reassurance and, no doubt, of a father substitute. Thus the time spent on the Isle of Man was not entirely wasted.

¶ I volunteered for the transport to Australia. I was convinced that no one would dream of sending us half-way round the world just to put us into another camp. There were not many volunteers. The *Arandora Star* with hundreds of my fellow internees had been sent to the bottom of the Atlantic not many days before. We did not understand why our housefather cried when he read out our names on the transport list.

¶ Half of the boys in our hostel, about forty, between the ages of seventeen and eighteen were interned to Australia. Later some of them joined the British Army, others settled in Australia and others were able to emigrate to the U.S.A. Some lost their lives after the boat that took them to internment was sunk.

¶ In all these war experiences my sympathies were all on the side of Britain which I had come to regard as my country.

OLDER CHILDREN IN WARTIME

¶ I was to go to an Orthopaedic hospital for children in Surrey where I was to become a probationer nurse. My name was one of the last to be called as we waited at the station and I felt utterly abandoned and lost. A lady finally put me on a train to Byfleet, where I was collected by a refugee girl who had been working in the hospital for some time. As soon as we got to the hospital I was fitted out with my uniform, shown my cubicle and taken in to tea. With all the excitement and upset of parting from my parents I had not been able to eat anything for three days and the sight of weak, milky tea which I tried to drink made me violently sick, in front of a dining hall full of people. Immediately after tea I was taken to a ward and my first job was to clean windows with methylated spirit. It took me about four weeks to settle down in my new surroundings. There were five more refugee girls and we were all very glad of each other's company. The English nurses must have looked on us as intruders. Being a foreigner in those days made one feel as though one were a freak and when I became a bit more friendly with one of the English girls and told her of what went on in Germany she obviously did not believe me. I got on very well with my little patients and tried out my very halting English on them. When war broke out things changed of course immediately. A few wards were prepared for wounded military personnel and the alien nurses were not allowed to go near any of those wards. As a matter of fact they were cordoned off. In June 1940 all the alien nurses were told to leave within 48 hours, as the place was being taken over as a military hospital. Luckily I had some friends in Nottingham who let me stay with them until I found another place. Aliens restrictions forbade my carrying on with my nursing training, but I managed to find a job as an assistant nurse in a private nursing home. There I became a jack-of-all trades; from kitchen work and looking after old people to even helping to bring babies into the world. Very good experience for a girl of sixteen, and all for 12s. 6d. a week. I stuck it for about six months and then, not realising what I was letting myself in for, took a job as nanny to a two-year-old boy, the son of very well to-do English parents. The little boy was extremely spoilt, and having had no previous experience with spoilt children I often lost my temper with him, usually just when his mother happened to listen at the door. After a few months the family decided to move and asked me to go with them. My duties increased sharply, and I was offered an increase in wages, which up till then were 15s. per week. The rise consisted of sixpence a week more and being very young and stupid I was highly delighted at such riches. In the meantime I had got in touch with some distant relations of mine in Manchester, who begged me to move there. The labour restrictions had been lifted and I would now be able to have a wider choice of jobs. I gave my notice to my employer and in return received a flood of abuse. The usual story about ungrateful foreigners. I had not thought it possible that a lady of her high breeding could use such language. I went to Manchester in 1942 to live in a Quaker hostel together with many girls of my own age and background, and felt happier than I had done for a long time, in spite of the very Spartan living conditions. First I had a job with a small Austrian firm as a leather worker, but when I heard of an opening in the millinery trade I grabbed it with both hands. My boss was an English Jew and he treated me well. I thoroughly enjoyed my work and designed my own hats eventually. I think my boss must have been pleased with me, he gave me a rise every three months. However, I had to register for war work and when the time came I chose to join the A.T.S. as a cook.

¶ As a boy of fourteen I was sent to work in some tailoring factory which I hated. I would have liked some more schooling, for which I was just too old.

¶ I now very much regret not having benefited from a proper training or completed my education. I came as a girl of fifteen and changed jobs a lot during my early years in this country. I felt very proud of the fact that I was independent and could earn my own keep quite well.

¶ When I was fourteen years old and it was time for me to leave school, there was the problem of starting me on a suitable career. Most of the lads who left our school became miners at the numerous nearby collieries. This I suppose was following in their fathers' footsteps. This was certainly not to be my calling. The

Committee had a special meeting and I was called in to them after a long wait. 'How would you like to become a printer?' the chairman asked cautiously. 'Yes,' I replied without hesitation, for I dreaded the prospect of the mines.

¶ There was little choice, so I decided to take up nursing. At fifteen I was not old enough to start a proper training, so it was arranged that I should go to a convalescent hospital for children in Birmingham. I met two or three other refugees there, which helped a great deal. After my arrival there war broke out and this meant evacuation of all the patients—but we soon had to cater for the 'overflow' of the children's hospital in the city. I found life very hard at first (as any girl would who took up nursing in those days) and it was rather painful to be called 'Jerry' by the patients. On top of this the nerve-wracking business of repeated air-raid warnings. But the staff were very kind and I managed to settle down after a while.

¶ It was only when I left my foster home at the beginning of the war that I became fully aware of my position as a refugee.

¶ When I had to leave my foster home at the beginning of the war I had no work permit for taking a job. After a whole day's consultation at Bloomsbury House I ended up at the Assistance Board and drew my first seven shillings and sixpence, weekly. This went on for some time until I was offered a job in a boarding house as a chambermaid for the wonderful sum of ten shillings a week. I would be on duty from 7 a.m. to 10 p.m. with two hours' break in the afternoon and I would share a room—with a matronly spinster who had seen better days—and who was to keep an eye on me. Although I was only seventeen and should really have stayed with my guarantors until I came of age, under the circumstances a work permit was arranged for me. This made me very happy and I was proud of my new status. Most of the guests in the boarding house were very kind to me and I made many friends. A music student who lived there with her mother and studied at the Academy allowed me to play her piano in my two hours off. I was taken to the open air theatre, to concerts and the cinema. My English improved rapidly, and except for my roommate, who completely disturbed my peace and aggravated my good life, all was well. I became friendly with the person who came to do the cooking and she suggested moving away from her parents' home and taking a flat together with me so that I could

enjoy a greater freedom and get away from my room-mate. This seemed a splendid idea: we would have a home and I could have a piano and study in the evenings. We found a basement flat in Kilburn which my friend furnished and together we bought a piano for three pounds. I worked in Corner Houses, in kitchens, in milk bars, in restaurants and as a lavatory attendant. Sometimes the shifts were so badly arranged that I would miss the last transport when I came off duty at midnight and would have to walk back again the next morning at 5 a.m. to be on duty at 6 a.m. Often I would not bother to go to bed but would sit up with some theory of music books to do some studying.

¶   It was decided that I should take a year's course in the Domestic Science Department of the local Technical College. I liked cookery very much and passed the City Guild's plain cookery examination with credit. I was seventeen years old when I took a job as cook at my old school (which took boarders as well as doing lunches for most of the pupils). I stayed there for only one term as it was much too hard work—a 13-hour day.

¶   When I left the hostel I found it difficult to manage on my own. I suppose theoretically someone was still responsible for me, but I didn't know who and didn't dare to try and find out—I had really had enough of being told what to do by absolute strangers.

¶   The feeling of being able to earn my own money and to be independent from Hostels and Committees was grand. Before long a friend and myself shared a room in Hampstead; we were both fifteen years old.

¶   When I discovered that I would be allowed to do other work I left my job as a domestic servant to become a shop assistant; eventually I worked in an office but at that time my English was not good enough. I earned 17s. 6d. out of which I paid 10s. for an attic room—the cheapest I could find. Even if I could have managed to live, there was still the problem of clothes—I was growing out of all the things for the sake of which my mother had sold the family silver. When I looked for a better job a fatherly man explained in the kindest possible way that girls of sixteen normally lived at home and could not expect to earn enough money to manage on their own, and why should he pay more to me than girls who spoke perfect English? I remember a later interview which I said that perhaps other girls who applied for such were not my equals in intelligence and upbringing. 'And h

were you when you left school?' I was asked. I burst out crying and ran away without answering: I had been thirteen.

¶ The Committee met to consider my case and I was told that as I was now sixteen years old they had decided to let me live under my own steam. But, I was warned, things were not going to be easy, for as I would now be taken off the register I could no longer be given any help. One kindly man followed me out of the room, patted my shoulder and said very sincerely: 'It's not really like that—if you need us just walk in.' Though I knew I could go back and promise to abide by their rules, I was determined never to have to do this. I found a better job and at week-ends I acted as an unofficial porter at Euston station. I would deny myself proper meals and buy loaves of bread. I found a cheap bed and breakfast place; the breakfast was good and would last me till evening. It was on my first Sunday at this boarding house that I encountered real hardship. I felt tired and had planned a long rest. In the afternoon I would go portering, but that morning I would return to bed after breakfast. At 10 a.m. the landlady knocked on the door to tell me that the gentlemen were expected to vacate their rooms during the day. Though life was very difficult at the time, today I get great satisfaction when I think that I managed to stand on my own feet.

¶ I banished any unease I occasionally felt about my future prospects. I had learned no trade, I was acquiring no professional qualifications.

¶ I asked at the labour exchange if they could find me a job in an office. They told me they couldn't because all the jobs going were of national importance and part of the war effort. But I would like to help the war effort, I said. 'Why should you?' they asked. 'You're a German. You *must* be on the other side.' I tried to explain that I had more reason to hate the Germans than they had, but even if my English had been better I don't think I could have convinced them.

¶ We had left Mr. Shaw because he had starved us. We had left although he had offered us a decent rise and filled our table until the buns almost rolled over the edges on the day we had given him our week's notice. Why? Because we were stupid and inexperienced and middle-class. At Mr. Low's we were starved worse. For a while we tried to restore at least some dignity to our meals. We came to an agreement with the third, a boy who sat with us at the labourers' table, to eat the thin slices of white bread in turn. But Mr. Low soon found out, cajoled or threatened the boy, and we had to grab again as fast as we could. It naturally shortened our mealtime breaks. He forbade us to buy pies in the village. 'People will think you don't get enough to eat here.' 'We don't.' He put his fist under Otto's nose and mine. 'I've seen you take photographs of yonder bridge. I've seen you make plans of the countryside. You are our enemies! You understand?'

¶ My relationship with my fellow workers was rather curious. In due course I was accepted, but rather in the manner of an associate than a full member. I was often told, without animosity, that I was not 'one of them'. (As least I wasn't classed as one of 'they'.) First of all I was a foreigner and a German at that. I was also a Jew. And as if that were not enough, in my general demeanour I was middle-class.

¶ At first I was regarded with some suspicion by the other workers, at least I imagine I must have been, but after a while I was fully accepted. I remember when my sister and I were bombed out and lost practically everything—for the second time one might say—the workers made a spontaneous collection amongst themselves and sent it to me with a note, asking me not to refuse it, as they 'would have done as much for anyone.'

II

¶ Being a refugee was very largely a case of being different and being made aware of that difference. The fact of not having a home was of paramount importance. A school is not a home; other people's houses are not home.

¶ I remember going through Stoke Newington during an air-raid and feeling so intensely alone that it was almost something tangible.

¶ I think the greatest hardship was not having a home. I had no relations at all in England and so in an emergency I had no one to turn to. Once, after starting a new job and while I was waiting for my first pay-packet, I really went hungry. Once I was ill in bed for two days before my landlady realised that something was wrong and came to find me. (I could have called her but I felt so awful about the situation that I did nothing about it.) What made me feel an outsider—an outcast, as if there were something wrong with me—was when I heard people talking on a Monday morning about what they had done over the week-end. They were girls of my own age and they all lived at home. I could not have felt more inferior about my position if it had been my own fault.

¶ Adolescence was difficult. I had no home, and consequently couldn't compete with the lives of other girls of my age.

¶ For three years after coming to this country I did not enter anyone's home. And when I finally did it was as a domestic servant.

¶ I had barely enough money to live (I existed mainly on Kellogg's Cornflakes for the first few months); as a boy of sixteen I lacked the experience to cope with such problems as laundry, proper food, clothing, etc. Nor did I know how to cope with the sudden complete freedom. What little money I had I spent mostly on the—to me—unknown wonders of the cinema. My mother had to work too hard for little money and had her own difficult problems and so at that time had not much influence on me and my way of life.

¶ I found the task of renting a room so awful that I took the first one I could have—which meant that I had to go through it all again before long. I found landladies always extremely suspicious that a girl of sixteen—I looked younger—should want to rent a room. I was invariably asked why I wasn't living with my parents—a question I could not answer without bursting into tears. Also, when it came out that I would have to register my address with the police, many landladies did not like this. One of them turned me away saying that she did not want someone with foreign habits in the house. To this day I don't know what she meant.

¶ Nearly always there seems to have been this feeling in the background of being slightly different and outside the gang. The friends I chose—or vice versa—seem also to have had this quality of being slightly apart from the crowd.

¶ I had many English friends, and did not particularly want the company of other refugees, but nevertheless felt that there was something lacking in many of these friendships. Although I wanted to be assimilated completely there was always this barrier.

¶ University added to finding one's feet. Students had heard of refugees and knew that they were Hitler's opponents or victims

rather than potential spies. Most of them treated me as their equal.
¶   University was better; suddenly, being different did not
matter, in fact it meant superiority. I still didn't fit in; my foreign
name and the fact that I was a very good student did not help me
merge in the mass of undergraduates. So I cultivated the
difference.
¶   At the university, there used to be a certain link, or feeling of
sympathy, between people who one found out were refugees.
There was almost a sort of Masonic set of signs that one looked
for or made, by intonation in sentences or something like that.
Openly it was very rarely discussed. The most one might say,
when seeing another one at a lecture on the Day of Atonement,
was: 'Fancy seeing you here, today.' And they would reply: 'Well,
fancy seeing you.' Then there might be the bare information
about when one came. You wouldn't necessarily chum up with
them, but there would be this certain sympathetic feeling. They
would have the same intellectual outlook, the same cynicism, or
the same sophistication, compared with English people, who had
had altogether perhaps more simple problems in life.
¶   Many refugees had practically no contact with English Jews,
though they may well have made many non-Jewish English
friends. This is probably because many of us came from rather
wealthy assimilated middle-class backgrounds whereas many of
the parents of our English contemporaries still lived in the slums
of the East End of London. I was once taken to tea to such a home
and it struck me for the first time that Jews could be poor and
lacking in the essentials of civilised living. The English Jewish
community is still very self-contained and very orthodox. To
them we seemed hardly Jewish at all.
¶   When I managed to move at last to a town where there was a
Jewish congregation I went to the synagogue on Friday night
almost as if I were going home. It was one of the greatest disap-
pointments of my life. It wasn't just that the service was very different—I didn't feel that I belonged amongst these people any
more than amongst the English. I suppose it was the Nazis who
had led me to believe that Jews were the same the world over.
Now I found out that it wasn't true.
¶   Living in a very small village (no bus or train service) whose
overall way of life was still almost feudal, with the squire, the
vicar, and a retired army officer directing the war effort, I found

myself almost immediately accepted as a member of the community (in spite of initial language difficulties). The squire's lady turned me into the local Red Cross collector for the Penny-a-week fund. The vicar gave me evening employment as his gardener for which he paid me quite well, supplied a substantial evening meal, threw in haphazard English lessons, and tried very half-heartedly, and unsuccessfully, to convert me. The younger villagers introduced me to their club, took me to the pub (two miles away), to the pictures (five miles away), and tried, in vain, to teach me to play cricket. I was often invited to their homes, joined their A.R.P. lectures, helped at scrap collections, annual garden fetes, and attended their weddings and the occasional funeral.

¶ I was introduced to the 'Austrian Centre' and became a member of the 'Young Austria' group. I joined their choir and we gave several quite successful performances, one even at the Wigmore Hall with quite an ambitious programme. As my command of English was apparently more fluent than that of the other members, I was soon delegated to contacting English youth groups and talking to them about occupied Austria and how 'democratic' and 'anti-Nazi' they really were. I was just sixteen and rather enjoyed my 'success', I suppose, but after a time I found myself unable to go along with the group's ideas or rather the ideas of the leaders of 'Young Austria'. It was of course for me and most of the other young people just a meeting place and we all came there for companionship mainly.

¶ The organisers of the 'Free German Youth' were mostly young people in their twenties or late teens, who had actively opposed the Nazis in Germany and had had to flee. I first came across the F.G.Y. in the summer of 1939 in a socialist youth camp near London. Some of the people had come with the children's transports and others were political refugees who had their own explanation of the causes of events in Germany. At the camp, activities included political discussions, hikes, amusements and much singing. The songs, folk songs, anti-fascist songs, Spanish civil war songs and some Russian songs with German text, sung with gusto to guitar accompaniment, had a great emotional appeal. Later a 'Free German Youth' choir was formed and gave public performances, for instance at the Everyman Theatre in Hampstead. For this we wore what we regarded as our uniform: white blouses and navy skirts. Other activities included helping in the

4*

youth centre, printing the paper, rambles with British organisations (e.g. Woodcraft Folk), attending first aid classes, joining
agricultural activities etc. The main criticism levelled at the
F.G.Y. was that it was communist. The organisers claimed that
it was non-political except for being anti-fascist, and that all view-
points were represented. While this may have been true, the
political refugees certainly had communist sympathies and aimed
at putting them across. Among all refugees at that time there were
three fundamentally different attitudes. The Zionist, the assimi-
late in the country where you are, and the go back and re-educate
the Germans schools of thought. The last was official F.G.Y.
policy. I was once in a train with two other girls, each of us repre-
senting one of these three views. While we argued, a British
schoolteacher entered the compartment and joined in the discus-
sion. 'Yes you are quite right, you must go away again,' she said.
'Foreigners weaken a nation, the Roman Empire collapsed because it was full of foreigners.' This new version of history startled
us and perhaps not many English people share these sentiments,
but quite a number could and still cannot differentiate between
the refugees of those days and other Germans.

III

¶ *Over one thousand young persons (including several hundred
girls) of the Children's Movement were members of the British
Forces, and thirty lost their lives.*

—They Found Refuge

One Boy's War
¶ I refused to join the Army while only the Pioneer Corps was
open to us, because I wanted above all to fight. Eventually I was
promised that I would be allowed to join a branch of the Fighting
Services. Much to my disappointment, after having volunteered,
I found myself in the Alien Pioneer Corps, after basic training,
testing Bailey Bridges. From there I volunteered for the Royal
Armoured Corps; before re-mustering to the R.A.C., the men of
our Company of the Pioneer Corps, all German and Austrian
Refugees, many of them having been in the Company since 1940,
when they joined straight from internment or Kitchener Camp,
and some having been at Dunkirk, were told to change their

names to English names, keeping initials wherever possible. We were also given false histories, false next-of-kin, etc. We were training for invasion and if we were caught in Germany we would not have been taken prisoners of war as English soldiers but would have been shot out of hand as traitors. One of the funniest incidents in my whole life was the Pay Parade following our change of names, when no one could remember his new name. Myer became Montgomery, Stuertzel became Stephens, and so on, and to top it all the last man on the Pay Parade every week, Zell, changed his name to Avent, so that he could be first to collect his pay.

At Farnborough I trained for three months as a tank driver, mechanic, wireless operator and gunner and was drafted to go to India, when volunteers were required to join a special unit being formed to become part of the 6th Airborne Division. Nearly half of this regiment were refugee boys, and sixty of them, including me, volunteered for this new unit which became the 6th Airborne Armoured Reconnaisance Regt., R.A.C. The Regiment's strength was just over 300, and amongst its members were ex-convicts, specially released for this unenviable job, adventurers, and refugees whose only aim was to be the first to kill Germans. At this time we felt that we had nothing to live for and were only too glad to die if we could kill a few Germans first.

At Larkhill, we had intensive training, Commando training, landing in gliders, war exercises, etc. in order to be ready for the invasion. When the invasion took place a large proportion of the refugee boys did not go, as it was felt they would be unstable at the first contact with the enemy, their hatred for the Germans being so great that it might not have been possible to keep them in check. My first chance came at Christmas 1944, when our unit was taken by sea to Ostend and used as ordinary tank and reconnaissance troops to repulse the Rundstedt offensive when they broke through the Americans in the Ardennes. Conditions were so bad that tanks could not be employed, owing to the ice and snow, and we were used as ordinary infantry. At times no rations could get through to us and on one occasion seven of us were down to our last tin of bully beef, which when opened was found to be green and completely uneatable. We were in Belgium for a month before we had a change of clothes. The Germans were eventually pushed back and we moved to a position on the Maas, opposite

Venlo, in Holland, which twelve of us held for a month. Our nearest units, also of twelve men, were three miles on either side of us. Our armaments consisted of three machine guns, rifles and sten guns and we surrounded our position with trip-wires which released flares if any Germans crossed the river. For a month, we were two hours on and four hours off duty, with the Germans on the other side of the Maas sending reconnaisance parties over most nights.

From Venlo we returned to England, re-grouped, and returned a month or so later, this time in tanks, landing in gliders on German soil at Wesel. After twenty-four hours of heavy fighting we established a bridgehead with the help of the U.S. 87th Air Brigade, who luckily landed in the same position instead of further south as intended. After mopping up the German paratroops who were there waiting for us, we advanced across Westphalia and north Germany until finally we reached the Elbe at Luneberg. At this time the Russians had not reached the Oder. Montgomery spoke to us at Luneburg Heath and promised that we would be the first troops to enter Berlin. For political reasons this never happened, and we did not cross the Elbe until late in April (maybe two weeks later, during which time we got the local Germans to re-paint our tanks and other vehicles). On 1st May I was among the first to meet the Russians at Wismar on the Baltic. Until 19th May, we were exchanging Polish, Lithuanian and Russian civilian forced labour and prisoners, for Dutch, French and Belgian handed over by the Russians. We were the first fighting unit to be flown back to England after the British prisoners of war had been repatriated.

After four weeks' leave—spent trying to re-adjust myself to normal, English, civilised conditions, after being in the thick of battle, licensed to kill, and willingly killing any S.S. men who were brought to us for this purpose by our English comrades, we returned to Larkhill where we started training for the airborne invasion of Malaya. The advance party left for India and we were on the boat ready to leave when the war abruptly finished in the East. It was decided by the War Office to send us to Palestine instead. Palestine Radio announced to the Jews that the 6th Airborne Division had managed to deal with the Germans and would now deal with the Jews. On arriving, we had a very cold reception. We were treated with contempt and our red berets were viewed in the way that the S.S. 'death' hat must have been viewed by the people in occupied Europe. This placed me in an invidious position: I was hated by the Jews of Palestine who could not recognise me as a Jew, and I was no longer trusted by the British because I was a Jew. From September 1945 until February 1946 I was in the worst predicament of my life, since I believed in the formation of a Jewish National State, but at the same time felt loyalty to the British Army. I could only visit my relations if I wore a black beret, instead of my red, as I would otherwise have placed their lives in jeopardy.

My friendships in the unit did not suffer and I still went out with the boys to cafés, or dancing, when not on duty at the police posts. The Jewish girls used to dance with me, but refused to dance with my non-Jewish friends, who had been through thick and thin with me.

Early in 1946 the Regiment was disbanded, most of the men transferring to the 3rd Hussars, who then took over our duties and were issued with red berets. A few men were left in the Headquarters Unit, three of us German refugees. Being a wireless operator, I worked in the telephone exchange at Sarafand, until it was realised that a Jew might not be reliable under certain circumstances. I and my two Jewish friends were then placed on guard duties—three 48-hour duties a week, with a haircut before each duty. When it came to the third duty I did not have my hair cut and was put on a charge by the sergeant-major. The officer dismissed the charge but told me to get a haircut. By this time it became abundantly clear that sooner or later things had to come to a head. A War Office instruction had gone out to all commanders before we even left for Palestine that no Jews or Moslems were to serve there. I, therefore, together with my two Jewish friends refused any further duties and asked for a Court-Martial, with the result that we were put on the next train to Cairo and, we thought, on our way home to England.

While in Palestine I contracted dysentery, living in the desert, and spent five weeks in a military hospital. My brother, being in Germany, found out the fate of my parents and relations. A detailed letter arrived while I was in hospital, causing a relapse in my condition, since when I have suffered repeatedly from this type of complaint.

Being among my own family in Palestine and meeting old

school friends who also lived there, I often spoke with them of the Jewish struggle for independence and was quite prepared, if asked, to desert and stay on in Palestine. One of my friends, a taxi-driver, was in the Hagana and he told me that I could further the cause better if I went to Cairo and got a job in the transit camp, the reason being that the Palestine Regiment was returning from Italy by way of Cairo for demobilisation. Along with this regiment were many men and women, in uniform but without any papers to get them beyond Cairo—men and women who had recently been released from concentration camps and were trying to get to Palestine. Arriving in Cairo, we were posted to the transit camp where I worked in the Pay Office and my friends went as interpreters into the desert to German P.O.W. camps. All the key jobs at the transit camp were held by Jewish members of the 6th Airborne Division—in the Quartermaster Store, Company Office, and, of course, Pay Office. Between us we were able to issue the necessary army papers to the would-be immigrants permitting them to 'return' to Palestine and providing them also with travel warrants. No other legal entry was possible.

I stayed in Cairo until January 1947, and then returned to England and was demobbed around July 1947. On arriving home—to my foster family—my first job was to report to the Aliens Office to re-register as a friendly enemy alien, although I had already applied for naturalisation whilst in Cairo. This came through at the end of August.

DEATH AND SURVIVAL

¶ 'I won't go!' he shouted at his parents. 'Why should I have to be pushed out on my own? I've done nothing wrong! I hate the Germans and I hate you!'

—The Story of Peter Cronheim

¶ When I came to England in 1939 I did not have any hopes or thoughts for the future. I was only eleven years old and it was all like an adventure to me, until I would be re-united with my parents. At that time I had no fears for their future or their lives.

¶ During the first few months of the war I managed to get some letters from my parents—not directly from Germany, but with the help of relations living abroad. But it was not until a year or two after the war that I heard of their fate. An aunt (my father's sister) had gone to Theresianstadt and was among those who were released by the Swiss at the beginning of 1945. She managed to contact me from Switzerland and told me that my parents were deported in 1941 and not heard of again. All my relations met with a similar fate, except an uncle who had emigrated with his family to Yugoslavia in 1934 and is now in Australia, and my brother, who came to this country in a children's transport two months before me.

¶ My father sent us loving postcards in bad English from Brussels and later in French from the Camp de Gurs where he found himself after fleeing to unoccupied France. About 1942 the letters ceased; enquiries by the Red Cross years later revealed that he had been taken to Auschwitz.

¶ Letters from Germany had stopped and presently I received my first Red Cross letter of twenty-five words from my parents, to which I could only reply twenty-five words once a month. . . . The Red Cross letters stopped coming from my parents and I had one, and then another, from my aunt Paula to tell me not to worry as my father and mother had come to stay for a while with her and she was writing for them. Another couple of letters like that and then these stopped as well, so that I was forced to fear the worst. Earlier there had been a massive raid on Dresden and I think about an equally big one on Leipzig, the neighbouring city where my parents had lived, so that I had been prepared in a background sort of way for my parents' death. When the letters stopped I did more or less accept without great shock and surprise that my family was dead. Yet I did not fully accept it for when in 1947 I received a letter from a friend of the family, more or less confirming their death in Auschwitz, it hit me very hard, when I would have thought I had by then anyway accepted the fact.

¶ I had heard via the Red Cross that there was not much hope of finding my parents alive. My brother and I travelled to Munich in the summer of 1949 with very mixed feelings. We were told there that our parents had been 'evacuated' to Theresianstadt and finally Riga. A transport which as far as we could gather never reached its destination.

¶ The death of my parents was only confirmed by the lack of information to the contrary some time after the end of the European war and somehow by then all the concentration camp stories had been and gone, and I suppose I had just quietly anticipated the outcome over some months. There was no sudden feeling of shock or loss. I have often wondered why, and can only assume that living without parents for five years had moulded an independent attitude to life, and so the loss found me immune.

¶ The news of my father's survival reached me a few days before that of my mother's death, early in 1945. One had slowly, over the preceding two–three years, forced oneself to get accustomed to the idea of never seeing them again. I was very excited about the news that my father was safe. The news of my mother's death left me, somehow, numb. It failed to register, although it was simply like a confirmation of what one had already known. At the same time, subconsciously, it was as if one had not lost but only mislaid one's mother and had to go on looking for her, even for the rest of one's life. Hence the succession of mother-figures. As it happened, I never saw my father again either, he survived Auschwitz but died in a Czech political prison in 1953.

¶ All their letters, through the Red Cross, said that they were well and contained some good advice regarding myself. Their letters stopped altogether in 1943 and all that my relations in Switzerland or I could find out was that my parents had been sent away on a 'transport' in 1943; that my father had died of a stroke on the train, and that my mother had been sent to Poland. To this day I am glad I never learned more exact details about my parents' fate. I have never wanted to know exactly what happened, and prefer to remember them as they were before the Anschluss. I have never been able to face with equanimity photographs, news-reels, etc. of concentration camps for fear of discovering my mother's fate.

¶ The end of the war meant that one had suddenly to come to terms with everything one had pushed away while it was going on. The continued anxiety about our families had been partly sub-merged in the sheer mechanics of coping with everyday life. Now the truth was inescapable. All my family with the exception of two young cousins who had survived Auschwitz had perished. The terrible facts of how it all happened were perhaps even more unbearable than death itself. Even now I feel unable to look them squarely in the face. Letters of surviving friends started to arrive and in the first summer months of 1946 my cousins came to Eng-land. Their hatred of the Germans was such that they could not even bear to hear a German word spoken (they were Czechs). I mention this visit because it meant a confrontation with the truth in its starkest colours and I was unable to stand up to it.

¶ I still sometimes imagine that it is possible for my mother to be alive somewhere (in spite of first-hand reports to the con-trary). Strangely enough I miss my mother progressively *more*, probably since I have become a mother myself, and I am fre-quently wondering how I behaved as a baby—but there is no one who knows, now.

About Felicia:
¶ *We thought that if her mother was coming we ought not to let her forget her, and so we said that if Mummy came Mummy would take her away, but nobody else would take her away, she didn't want to go, she didn't like strangers, and so we said, well, nobody else would take her, only Mummy. There was a photograph, a little snapshot we had of Mummy, we kept that in her bedroom, we tried to keep her mother in her mind, thinking that would be the best thing to do, but of course when eventually the news came that they were all killed, we thought we'd better tell her. So I told her one night.*

She said: 'All my family? My mother and my father and my brother and my grandmother and my cousins and my aunties—everybody?'

And I said: 'Yes, Felicia, I'm afraid so.'

She said: 'Oh, now I can stay with you.'

She put her mother's photograph in a drawer and she has never looked at it since. I leave it there. She says there is no point in having that now. The tragedy was that she heard the news with relief. There is no question about that. She was afraid that her mother was coming and now that she knew that she wasn't coming she was relieved.

For nights after that she used to cry, after she'd gone to bed. She wouldn't tell us, she never does talk to you, she didn't tell us at all what was wrong. Until eventually I said: 'Look here, what is the matter?'

And she said: 'I don't want you to die.'

She was then nine years old.

¶ One day when my sister and I got home from school we were told to sit down and were given a letter from our parents. The first news for years! The first intimation that they were still alive. They wanted us home again. It was as though the whole house rocked. We were flabbergasted and horrified. No! We didn't want to go. We belong to you, Aunt and Uncle! We can't go! So it was left to Uncle to write this difficult letter to suggest that we finished our education here and did not go through another upheaval. To which they agreed.

¶ My non-Jewish mother and baby brother had been left behind in Germany until it was too late to get them out. After the war my father managed to get to Germany with the Americans, as translator at Nuremberg, etc., and was able to visit my mother and brother, to augment their near-starvation diet in Berlin. We did not succeed in getting them over to England until 1948.

¶ I saw my mother after the war when I was seventeen, in Holland. The situation was highly charged emotionally—Mother wanting to protect me and make up for the long absence and I wanting to be independent. I found it difficult to establish a relationship; I felt guilty about this but couldn't do much about it. After all I had found a mother-substitute during my formative years. Mother felt most ambivalent towards the people who had brought me up—jealous because of my alienation and grateful because I was fit and well. My sister who was older by four years and who was with me was able to get on much better and I think helped my mother. Both subsequently went to the United States and I opted to stay in England to finish my education, but because of my marriage and general reluctance to go never followed them.

¶ A year before I was due to write the thesis for my Ph.D. I managed to arrange for my parents to come from Shanghai. I very much resented the sense of obligation which made me take this step and I did not really make our new life together particularly happy. My father died in 1952 and my mother returned to Vienna and her friends and relations in 1955. Every now and again I take the family there or she comes here and we spend a delightful few weeks of constant bickering.

¶ In 1947 my parents came to England for a holiday. It was a most marvellous summer and they had a really good recuperation after their dreadful ordeals and sufferings and privations. Uncle and I drove to London to meet them. It was arranged that I should be wearing a blue Harris tweed costume and Uncle sunglasses. It was pouring with rain and Uncle certainly was conspicuous. We waited for hours and ran from platform to platform as different trains arrived. Then suddenly we saw them! My parents, after eight years of separation from them; I had been eight years old, now I was nearly seventeen. At the first moment we felt strange, then quickly everything was all right and we understood each other, though my German came so slowly and was very limited. After the summer holidays my parents went home and we carried on with our English lives. We had had a few disagreements with my father and misunderstandings with my mother. Our ways of life were really different. When my father was annoyed with us he said: 'Uncle must smack you.' Of course, by this age we were never smacked—indeed, corporal punishment had been rarely inflicted. There could not have been a greater difference between my father's excitability and Uncle's extremely English 'keep calm and cool' attitude. By inheritance, I have my father's temperament, by environment since the age of eight I had calm, quiet and dignified behaviour shown me. My parents have been over to England several times to stay with us, but I have never been back to Vienna. Although it is rather sad to have grown so much away from my parents, I do feel that Auntie and Uncle are more my parents than my own. We see as much as we can of them and they are always available to give help or advice if they are asked. I feel that we were very lucky to be sent to them and that we probably had a better education and grounding to face life than we might have done had we not been refugees.

¶ All during the war I did not hear any more from home and did not know whether my mother and sister were alive or not. It took some time after the war to find out that my mother and sister were alive, and also that we had a brother. About two years ago, Mutti came to England to visit us, it was the first time in 24 years that we met. Of course we were very happy to see each other and had lots to talk about, but our lives are so far apart—Mother is very Austrian and I'm all English.

¶ My mother (non-Jewish) still lives in Hamburg. We visit each other occasionally but the years we were separated have proved too great a gulf to be bridged.

¶ My father returned to Germany from America ten years ago and consequently we are able to see him for ten days or so each year—but by the time we are starting to make any real contact it is time to separate again.

¶ In August 1946 and again in the following year I went to Prague for holidays with my father in our old flat. I now began to take in what he had gone through during the intervening years. He had led a hunted life for two years until the inevitable concentration camps, and had spent three months at Auschwitz, where he had been selected for labour rather than the gas chambers. After he had recovered in a Russian hospital he made his way back to Prague. He appeared to be the sole survivor of all our relations who had stayed behind. Wisely and selflessly he always advised me to return to England.

¶ Our father was a pastor of the confessing church, and was persecuted from about 1936 onwards, spending the war years in Dachau. Our mother was killed in the fighting in March 1945 and our father was killed in a road accident shortly after his release from Dachau. My younger brother and sister who had stayed with my mother still live in Germany, my other sister and I have remained in England. We would have to interpret if all four of us were ever together, which we have not been since 1952.

¶ I met my brother for the first time since leaving Vienna nine years before. I was terribly nervous about the re-union, but it went off well, though I was glad my husband was with me to give me moral support. He and my brother got on well together and the ice was soon broken.

¶ Why my brother and I were not sent to England together I don't know. He came over a few weeks later and was sent to a different hostel in another town. I did not see him again until 1943. It was really tragic that we were separated as I'm sure, had we been together, it would have made a lot of difference to me. We have spent very little time together since then. My brother went to Israel in 1948, and we have only met once since.

¶ When we came to England, he looked to me, his elder brother, to replace his parents and I felt that he always held a grudge against me because I couldn't give him the guidance in life that he needed, since I had to make my own way in the world, and find my own feet. He married in 1952 and emigrated to Canada two years later and in 1964 we met again for the first time in ten years. For the first time, I feel that we are no longer strangers.

¶ *She and her sister continued to quarrel and never grew close in any way; they are still, in a sense, mere acquaintances. This can be attributed in part to the desire of the younger one to shed all her foreign connections.*

¶ My parents and younger sister had gone to Chile just before the outbreak of the war, but as I was perfectly happy, my parents decided to leave me in England to finish my education. The war, of course, made it impossible for me to join them. In 1953 my sister came to England on a study course. She was only nine years old when I left Germany and I found that having been brought up in completely different surroundings, we had neither values nor interests in common. When I saw her again in 1959 just before her marriage we got on very much better and have ever since kept up a lively correspondence. My mother came to visit us for the first time in 18 years in 1956, and it proved a difficult time for all of us. My family at that time spoke little German and my mother of course little English. The children were too old to attach themselves immediately to their grandmother; as my daughter, then aged twelve, expressed it: 'I know she is your Mummy, but to me she is just a lady.' Perhaps we had expected too much of this reunion. I had always been very attached to my father and when he came to stay with us in 1958 we seemed to fall back into some sort of intimate relationship. Of course he was less demanding than my mother and put himself out to please us or at any rate not to criticise my less than perfect housekeeping. When both my parents visited us just over two years ago we all very much enjoyed their brief stay. I went to visit my parents in Chile in 1959 to attend my sister's wedding. This has been the only time our family was all together since 1938. As neither my husband nor my children had come with me the clock seemed to have been turned back. My father was well-established again, having taken his medical qualifications again, and I loved the fuss and attention I got. The contrast between my sister's and my wedding was striking, of course, and her state of housekeeping was certainly more comfortable than mine. In fact the contrast between our two lives shows very clearly the consequences to me of having been separated from my parents at the age of fifteen.

¶ I have one cousin (and she has me) with whom I had my first reunion last year, a very joyous occasion. She lives in Israel, and we hope it won't be another twenty-five years before we see each other again.

¶ In 1947 I had news of my parents' death, and also of my aunt's survival, though ill and old. This did give me new heart, and wading through all sorts of regulations and restrictions I finally got permission for her to come over. I was working and could support her, and she could stay with my foster parents, at first anyway. It was with much joy that I looked forward to her coming: I would learn something of my family and be in a sense reunited and not feel quite so alone. The plane ticket was bought and the seat booked and I remember walking down a peaceful high-banked English country lane, thinking manfully that I would bring my old aunt over to the peace and serenity of lovely England, and look after her after all the terrible things that had happened. She had made her way from a Russian detention camp at the age of seventy-two into the British Zone to friends. They were in touch with me and in spite of their lack of everything after the war they took her in and cared for her till she could come to me in England. But it was not to be. She died two days before she was due to catch the plane, and that final loss really brought home to me the loss and separation and loneliness I had come to accept almost as normal.

FACING THE FUTURE

I

¶ Bitterness about lost opportunities is only second to that about having been cut off so suddenly and for ever from one's family. Loss of education, from about a year before I left Germany to nearly another year after coming to England, plus the months wasted while having to learn English when I finally did go to a village school before I could again being to have even basic education—this loss made it extremely difficult for me and of course many others to get anywhere at all in later life. One did not appreciate it then, but this double loss of parents and education inevitably wrenched one's life to a lower and extremely limited path. It put all but the most outstandingly brainy years behind in the struggle for some sort of position in life. In my case it was a struggle I never caught up with. Being now of a studious nature I realise intensely the unalterable loss of education when I was put to work at fifteen in a flour mill. It took years of study, some intermittently, and lots of weary keeping at it with many lapses, to learn anything at all, and although I now have a reasonable position, it is not what I could have had and been, with only an ordinarily reasonable education.

¶ When I came to London my foster parents sent me to school to learn English. This school had a secretarial department, and I also learnt typing, book-keeping, etc. When my parents came just before war broke out, my foster parents persuaded my father to let me stay on at school a bit longer, but after a further term there he insisted that I should leave at once and find a job, in order to contribute to the family finances. I had to leave since my foster parents (who were willing to pay) felt that they could not interfere.

¶ I left my foster home to live again with my parents in 1945, and for the next two years or so continued to go to grammar school. I took School Certificate and gained distinctions in all subjects. My headmistress thought I should try to get to university, and I had three months in which to 'do' Latin from scratch,

after which I got a distinction in this subject too. But my parents'
circumstances then made it necessary for me to begin earning a
living.

¶ My headmistress strongly urged that I should stay on at
school and take Higher School Certificate. I should have loved to
go to university eventually, but there were many snags: being a
foreigner I wasn't eligible for a state scholarship and neither my
foster parents nor I knew of the Senior City Scholarship for which
I may have been eligible; furthermore my foster parents were not
prepared or could not afford to pay for me at university. I left
school at sixteen.

¶ I was sent to school; while the other girls seemed very young
and childish, I was not unhappy and have ever since been grateful
for the opportunity to take my matric. I had been brought up to
think of becoming a doctor and to follow my father. This was
quite out of the question now, and when it came to a choice of
career I simply had no idea what I wanted to do. I hated leaving
school and would have dearly liked to go on to university, but did
not like to even mention this to my guardian. Rather too late did
I discover that the Refugee Committee would have financed my
studies, but the Essential Works Order had come into force by
then and I had to comply with it.

¶ I feel that the sketchiness of my education and the wrong
direction it eventually took was due as much to the war as to any
lack of interest on the part of my foster parents. They did, after
all, do the best they could for me, and their daughter left school at
an earlier age than I.

¶ When my foster sister and I were both nearly fourteen, her
mother thought that we might as well go to a commercial school
and learn shorthand and typing, a plan with which we fully
agreed. All we wanted to do was to start work and earn some
money. We went to this school for two months. I didn't like
shorthand and typing much, however, and soon began to worry
about my almost total lack of education. After a lot of brooding
about this, and making a tremendous effort (I have always found
it rather difficult to talk to people on really important matters), I
asked my foster mother if we couldn't go back to grammar school
and she agreed.

¶ Education was of course of prime importance to me because
I was a refugee. One knew that to one who was an outsider edu-

cational qualifications were of more than ordinary importance. The magic word 'matric' had been known to us even in Germany as something one would have to aim at, and having been expelled from school in November 1938 I was in an unusual way excited and pleased to be able to go to school again. Like many other refugee boys and girls I became no doubt something of a swot and no doubt did better at school and university than I would have done in normal circumstances.

¶ If one is to attempt at all to pinpoint the moment I stopped being a refugee this was probably it: the day I passed my School Certificate. From then on I grew increasingly confident and secure and looked to the future with a reasonable amount of optimism.

¶ Neither my sister nor I spoke English when we arrived in this country, being very young, but after a spell at the local elementary school we both won scholarships to grammar schools. I attended one from 1943 to 1950, taking part in dramatic and musical activities. This was a period of quite severe adjustment difficulties for me, and in retrospect I think that I suffered from a sort of persecution complex and quite acute inferiority feelings. But in spite of this I formed friendships, some of which have stood the test of time even to this day. At school I was a house prefect and then a school prefect, won a state scholarship and an open scholarship to Oxford, and the school's Headmaster's and War Memorial Prize.

¶ I went to university and began at last to feel that I was responsible for what I made of my life, an exciting discovery. It had taken a long time to accept that my parents were dead, and that family life as it had been would never return, and once this fact was firmly established it seemed possible to make a new start.

¶ At university I studied mathematics. In July 1948 I shared the Dalton Mathematics Scholarship—an honour more than financial gain—and in 1950 I passed the B.Sc. examination with first class honours. I did all the things a normal undergraduate does. I then went to Cambridge to do research on Theory of Numbers. This led to a Ph.D. in the summer of 1953.

¶ On the advice of my teachers I took the entrance examination to Royal Holloway College, because this was a women's residential college and I had nowhere to live. I did not attempt Oxford or Cambridge because I could not afford a third year in the 6th form. While I was at college, my mother, my brother and I were naturalised. I felt resentful that the British Council should send me letters for foreign students; I did not consider myself one of them. On the other hand, I did not feel English. Before I was naturalised, a fellow student sitting next to me asked: 'Are you English?' 'No, German.' 'Oh, I'm History,' she said. I had gained an exhibition to Royal Holloway. At the interview the Dean asked me if I could not be persuaded to do German; my subsidiary German paper had been so good. I never considered this for one moment. At an interview for the Institute of Education, I was asked why I wanted to teach English and not German and took this as an affront.

¶ In 1943 I started at a grammar school; there I passed my matric with a distinction in English language, and my Higher School Certificate examination. I obtained an open exhibition to university in 1948, and from that year until 1951 I read English Honours. I became a teacher at a secondary modern school and was made head of the English department in 1960.

¶ At no time in my professional career has my background been a hindrance, at least I don't think so. If it has stopped any advancement that I wanted this knowledge has been kept from me. Perhaps it's because I have been mostly in an academic world where the main criterion is how well one does one's job.

¶ Starting with nothing, I had the chance to get ahead through scholarships etc. and now earn an excellent salary and do a full-time educational job as professor of Theoretical Magnetism.

¶ During the Blitz in 1940 the Home I was in was evacuated to Devon. About a dozen of us won scholarships to Tiverton Grammar School, and in retrospect I realise that this school had more influence and effect on us than can be conceived. The teachers overcame all our psychological impediments, the Home's religious zealotry and the dislocation of war, and moulded us into young men who would fit easily into English society. The headmaster, Mr. Duffin, was a strict, likeable, sensitive man who loved boys and thought that he owed a debt to the young Jewish refugees in his school. Some of us had suffered more than others from our disjointed education, but all the erstwhile refugees who attended the grammar school eventually graduated. All but one did so by working their way through university, i.e. by supporting themselves. This, incidentally, to the unfeigned delight of Mr. Duffin, who considered that he had made us, as indeed he had.

¶ At Oxford, where I was an undergraduate from 1951 to 1955, I did well academically, but the unsolved legacy of a turbulent childhood and the resultant emotional problems made me subject to moods of alternative depression and uncontrollable rage. I began to seek out psychiatric treatment from 1950 on, but nothing was seriously achieved in this line until I underwent a prolonged course of psychiatric counselling and analysis during my years as a post-graduate student at an American university between 1958 and 1963. Between leaving Oxford in 1955 with a B.A. in Modern Languages and History and returning to train for a university career in 1958, I spent eighteen months with the B.B.C. in London and in a private bank. At that time I had no very clear idea really of what I wanted to do. I left for America in 1957 to work for my Ph.D. in Russian History with the promise of a teaching assistantship and a Ford Foundation Fellowship, but was still very withdrawn in my inter-personal relationships and tending towards suspiciousness and irritability. While I was in the U.S.A. I became an American citizen but this has not meant that I have given up my British nationality. I returned to this country at the beginning of 1964, with my graduate studies completed, and am now a university lecturer in History and very happy in my position.

¶ 1941: Living at a hostel I started work as a learner dressmaker. I did not like the work very much but became interested in working and living conditions of the workers and the effect these conditions had on them.

Later in 1941 I decided to become a nurse. This was an old childhood wish. I had always been attracted by social work—and medicine. My parents were deeply involved in social work within the Jewish community of our town and many of our friends were doctors.

Late in 1941 I started as a student nurse in a Fever Hospital. The first three months went well—I was enthusiastic—I was liked—then I left after another two months because I was unable to cope with the disciplinary actions taken to regulate the student nurses' life.

I then became a parlour maid to a wealthy Englishwoman living in the country. After three months there I decided that hospital work was after all better than this.

I re-applied to another hospital—again a Fever Hospital—and

was accepted (they were so short of willing student nurses). As usual I started off quite well. After eight months I feared the preliminary examinations which were looming ahead, I resented the discipline and I felt that I was not doing any real war work. I left from one day to another, for which the matron has never forgiven me. (I am not surprised.)

I then started work in a war factory—precision work—turning spindles on centre lathes, etc.—and felt better. I felt that I was in the war effort and participating as much as I could.

1943: Had another try at hospital work—because I felt that war work would not give me a profession. Recommenced at yet a third hospital—this time a General Hospital—as a student nurse —and alas—after another three months capitulated; and again, it was I believe the discipline I could not tolerate.

1943–45: Back to war work in a factory.

1945: I felt that I must do something about a profession and decided I would start in a nursery. I took my nursery nursing training, qualifying in 1947.

In 1947 I went to Hamburg and worked for a time for the British War Trial Commission. My work was mainly office work.

1951: I commenced student nurse training at a London General Hospital. I qualified in 1954 with S.R.N. qualification and the gold medal of the training school. I accepted the discipline easily—made friends very easily—was very popular throughout the training period—and altogether felt very much happier.

November 1954: I wrote to my father in New York telling him of my success with a certain amount of pride. (My mother had been killed at Maidaneck—1942?) To this date I don't know whether he received this letter. However, I had a letter from him around the same date (the letters must have crossed) informing me that he intended to marry again. This news hit me so hard that I wrote to him bitterly complaining of being left alone in the world etc. He never answered this letter or any other but died in the middle of the following January.

December 1954: I started a deep depression. Instead of going to see a doctor I wrote despairing letters to some friends. Since I always appeared to be a cheerful person nobody took these letters seriously. Then after the news of my father's death I made a suicide attempt—and as a result of this landed in a mental hospital as a patient for about two months. I had little treatment there—worked a bit in the ward—did some pottery—reading—and felt much better eventually.

1955–57. I first went back to my training school to work as a staff nurse for a while—then decided to do my midwifery training part 1. Again I had no difficulties with either examinations or with colleagues, senior or junior, and was quite satisfied with my progress.

After finishing part 1 I went to Israel for a holiday. I was a member of a Zionist youth organisation while still at home and Israel had always interested me. I spent six weeks there and decided to go back to London and finish my second part in midwifery and then go out to Israel.

1957: I qualified as a midwife and left for Israel as arranged. I worked first in a kibbutz, learning the language, doing some agricultural work and later on was appointed as an acting sister in charge of an orthopaedic ward in a big military hospital.

While in Israel my old personal difficulties returned and new difficulties arose. I found the language hard and difficult to learn—I had a working knowledge, but it left me out of Israel's political and cultural life. I was thrown back for purposes of social intercourse on to my own and adopted cultural groups—the Germans and the English. The Sabras I found difficult to get on with. I found the effect of the different ethnical groups and the influence they had on one another in Israel as disappointing as any racial discrimination in any other country and decided that if I had to be an alien, I might as well be an alien where I had so far made reasonable progress in being accepted—namely in England. In Israel I would have had to start all over again.

In 1959 I came back to England to take the Health Visitor's Course and qualified in 1961.

1961–63: I worked as a health visitor in London, liked the job and the scope of work. While doing this I became particularly interested in teaching. I started to organise and take mothercraft and fathercraft classes and taught health and hygiene in a primary school.

1963: I applied to a teacher's training college and was accepted, and because of my previous professional qualifications only had to do one year.

1964: I qualified and became assistant lecturer at a technical college, teaching Liberal Studies.

1965: I have the intention of taking an A-level this year—as I would like to do a degree in B.Sc. (Soc.).

¶ 1939—40: I attended grammar school, and when my foster parents moved to another town I went to the technical college there for one year secretarial course.

1942–43: I worked as a typist in the technical college and attended evening classes. In June 1943 I obtained London Matriculation.

1943: I left my foster parents and lived on my own in another town for the following three years working at various jobs and attending the university there in my spare time.

1943–44: I worked as typist full-time, attending evening classes only. Obtained London External Intermediate. On the strength of that I taught part-time at a private girls' school, attending both evening and day lectures.

1945–46: I attended the university full time financed by studentship, grant by International Student Service and loans. Obtained B.Com. degree (London External).

1946–48: worked as research assistant in Economics Department of another university.

1948–50: worked as research assistant in National Institute of Economic and Social Research.

1951–56: research worker at Midland university. Wrote Ph.D. thesis.

I married in 1948. I have four children born between 1955 and 1963, and since 1956 I have undertaken no regular paid employment. However, in the last few years I have begun to do rather more voluntary work. I am a member of the Youth Club Committee and the Youth Service Committee of our town, and also of the Governing Bodies of the local College of Further Education and of the Girls' Grammar School.

II

Man consists of three elements: body, soul and passport.
—A Russian Saying

¶ Originally we had come into the country on a temporary basis and throughout the war no official announcement was ever made that we would eventually be allowed to stay. My brother joined the United States Army and after ninety days be became an American citizen. My cousin, who happened to have a Polish passport, could join a fighting force. But because I had a German passport I was not even given a rifle until 1941. Frenchmen who joined the Free French in England were promised that they could if they wanted to take British nationality after the war. No such promise was made to us and 'German' servicemen who were discharged became again enemy aliens under police supervision, though they might be drawing a British Army Pension. Right till the end of the war there was no security, you might say, of tenure.

¶ Naturalisation—the first step to establishing roots.

¶ I was naturalised under a special scheme introduced after the war for young people like me who had gone into foster homes and whose parents were dead, as we could not be legally adopted until we were British subjects.

¶ I married an Englishman when I was eighteen and from then on I ceased to be a refugee. I became a British subject on my marriage and no longer had to conform to restrictions imposed on aliens. My life then took the path of many other young wives during wartime.

¶ I stopped feeling a foreigner when I joined the Army—even the Pioneers because you wore British uniform, what unit you were in doesn't matter. Once you get naturalised you're as good as the next man. You pay your rates, you pay your taxes, you can vote, you can sit on a jury, you can do anything you like.

¶ In 1947 I asked the Czech Embassy to revalidate my expired passport. The official's mistrust, his probing questions—searching for what?—made the interview end disastrously with my tearing the old passport in half and throwing it at him. It was then I sought naturalisation. The Home Office official was an ex-rugger blue, and we discussed a recent international at great length. It was only afterwards that I realised how informative the interview must have been—more subtle, and much more effective, than the other one.

¶ Naturalisation was something I had forgotten about until the early 1950s, when not being legally British was a hindrance in business. Until then I had virtually overlooked the fact that I was still technically 'German'. Thus I embarked upon this legalisation of something that I had already established in fact with all those around me.

¶ My wartime residence in the U.K. was not taken into consideration when I applied for permission to file my application for naturalisation. This I could only do on the fifth anniversary of my last entry into the U.K. The certificate of naturalisation was granted in 1957, but first I had to renounce my Czech citizenship. By that time, I was the father of two daughters. British-born and educated, our daughters know only one country, and to them Czechoslovakia is, to quote the words of a British Prime Minister, 'a small far away country', and those who live there are 'people of whom we know nothing'. This is our home, this is where we belong.

¶ I am naturalised British and consider this state an understatement of my actual position, which is that I am no different in any essential respect except accident of birth from any other British citizen.

¶ I have never become naturalised. I was still under eighteen when my father was naturalised and we were told that I would have to apply again myself later. I am married to an Englishman, that does not automatically make me English—that was stopped after the war, when so many German girls married British soldiers. During the war, I wanted to join the Wrens, I wanted to join them so badly and I couldn't have done even if I had been naturalised then—you still had to have British-born parents. So I don't see that it matters. To my sister, being naturalised mattered terribly. She wanted to be British, and that was that. But I think that it is a mere formality. I feel so strongly English that it would make no difference to me. I am married to an Englishman and my three children are English-born. So that satisfies me.

¶ I was naturalised in 1947, but must admit that my change of nationality has meant little to me, a mere technical formality. I do not 'feel' either English or German; indeed my experiences have made me acquire a determinedly international outlook, and I am suspicious of most forms of so-called patriotism.

¶ Naturally we shall always remain 'naturalised' citizens, the fact of not having been born in Britain will always make us somewhat 'different'.

¶ My father, sister and myself were naturalised after the war, but I nevertheless continued to feel that I really was a refugee. From time to time people would ask where I came from, or when I was returning 'home', and then the awfulness of the situation would be brought home to me once more. Some refugees no doubt came to terms with it, but I never could, and to this day I resent having my provenance enquired into, I suppose because it reminds me that I am different from other people, or at any rate in the minority. I did not meet with any unpleasantness on this account, either during the war or after, but if anything did go wrong—if I didn't get the job, or promotion I wanted, I frequently believed, rightly or wrongly, that this was due to my being a foreigner.

¶ I did not become naturalised until my marriage in 1951. This is after all a mere formality, I am no different now to the 'bloody foreigner' I was before—I still have my accent, I am only British and never English, and even my passport gives the game away by stating my place of birth.

¶ I feel at home in England and I feel that I have been accepted for what I am. True enough I am still different from the ordinary run of people, despite having become a British subject, and the man in the street still becomes aware of it when we have closer contact.

¶ I have now been married for fifteen years and have two children, and we are comfortably off. But in all these years of British Citizenship we find that whereas we certainly don't feel like refugees any more, we don't seem to be fully integrated either. It takes more than one generation to do that.

III

¶ Some of us who had come as older children founded the *Hyphen* in November 1948 for those who in their everyday activities had been fairly successfully integrated into British life, but who, by virtue of their earlier education and upbringing, felt that the group could constitute a link between the culture they had brought with them and the way of life into which they were gradually being absorbed.

We began with numerous lectures by outside speakers, English and refugees, frequent rambles, socials and dances, study groups, a drama group, the latter confined chiefly to play-readings of English and German literature, and some welfare work for the benefit of sick and aged refugees.

In order to justify our existence as a group, we had intended at the outset to be a link between the two extremes, the native of this country and the un-integrable foreign immigrant. For this 'link' one of the more poetic members suggested the name *Hyphen*. Since then its age limits have been extended, mainly upwards. Its affluence, too, has grown with that of the society in which we live, but on the whole a little faster. Its membership has kept remarkably steady in number—about eighty—though the type of members has changed greatly. Whereas initially the *Hyphen* consisted of Jewish refugees with activities designed to be of interest to that type of person, there was a gradual influx of British-born Jews and even of British-born non-Jews, many of whom have contributed towards our activities.

The cultural events of earlier years have given way to social ones of various kinds. As members graduated from 'digs' to flats and then to houses of their own, they threw open their homes, and the various 'at Homes' on the *Hyphen* programmes are by now the most important features which help to keep up a connection between the older members and the more recent ones. Many of these homes are the direct result of acquaintances originally made in the *Hyphen*.

FACING THE PAST

I

¶ I had remembered him as a kindly chap who took an interest in us boys, so naturally and naïvely I went up to him with a warm greeting. After a time lag of over four years and all that had passed he scarcely remembered me, and when he did he said, 'Oh yes, you are the German boy, aren't you?' in front of all those people at the end of the war. It was not unfriendly or friendly, just neutral and without any consideration. I made my escape as best I could and felt very upset for a long time.

¶ At the end of the war my attitude towards Germany was complex, tortured and muddled. From within I had dissociated myself from everything German. I no longer regarded myself as German and I strongly resented that others should still do so. I cursed my accent which prevented me from hiding my German origin. Nothing enraged me more than to be told 'once a German, always a German', and at the same time I emotionally agreed when, more often than not, the same people followed up one hackneyed phrase with another: 'the only good German is a dead one'. In the arguments and discussions which usually followed such remarks, I often found myself 'running with the hare and hunting with the hounds'.

¶ I did not choose them and they almost abolished me. I cannot feel bitter at this old injustice committed against an infant. I expect I would have become a well-integrated German had I not been Jewish—but I regret the intolerance, stupidity and cruelty. . . . This is an old wound, and I am of the generation in whom the wound is healed. I do not hover at the frontier listening for news, I have a mild interest and a mild contempt. Faintly, I am inferior to them, for I was marked reject, however hard I exceed elsewhere. Naturally there is a painfulness—but it is slight, and distant in time. I am guilty of differentness—this is a true guilt and I cannot feel great rancour against those who punish such an offence; but I reserve a hate for those who have created that differentness—they were anonymous and are mainly dead. Let me admit to a certain confusion of emotion on this point.

¶ I found it very difficult to get rid of my German passport; in the end, by special request on my part, the Army 'lost' it for me—my sergeant at the Training Barracks took it and handed it in to the Orderly Room. . . . Why didn't I simply throw it away?

¶ During the war years we often said: 'We're not Germans, we're refugees from Nazi oppression.' In Germany I was baptised and brought up as a Christian. They said we were Jewish and I see nothing to be ashamed about and I get very cross if someone tries to hide the fact of it. My father is a Jew, so I'm half Jewish, but the only difference it makes is that I know something about the Jewish religion and another doesn't. In a sense it makes a difference because of what happened to us, the lives we had to lead. If anyone asks me am I Jewish I say yes. But I don't mean this as a nationality. If anyone said to me every German was a Nazi, then I would explain to him how could that be—I was a German in those days.

¶ I evolved a hundred and one answers to the question: 'And where do you come from?'—one true, one false, and ninety-nine evasive. For a long time, I found saying that I was Jewish just as difficult as saying that I was German.

¶ I don't mind now admitting that I'm a German—where you're born is a circumstance beyond your control and I'm not ashamed of it any more. But I used to be ashamed of it. I used to hold back with people until they knew the facts about me. I always told them right at the start—it was something I had to get over.

¶ I find that even now I only tell people that I originally came from Germany, or discuss the whole question, when I already know them very well. I can see that it's a sort of accolade of 'real friendship' that I bestow.

¶ I still have an accent, so that people will ask me: 'Where do you come from?' Sometimes I am self-conscious about this, and hesitate before I speak to people I have not met before.

¶ Despite the fact that I have become completely anglicised, or perhaps because of it, I do not talk readily to people (except very close friends) about my origins. I want to be thought of as completely English. Unfortunately I still cannot knit the English way, and for that reason will never knit in public. I suppose this is because I don't want to be 'different' from *real* English people. I never think of my birthplace as 'home' now and never refer to it as such.

II

¶ Linguistically my naturalisation is very thorough. People tell me I have no accent. I was eight when I came, my brother was eleven and a half and he never lost a trace of a continental accent. What helped in my case was that I spent over a year in a boarding school where it was forbidden to speak German. It was considered unpatriotic.

¶ I consciously kept my mother-tongue, with the result that I never completely lost my accent in English. Although I was only twelve years old when I came, I feel closer to the cultural traditions of Central Europe than of England.

¶ During the war I refused to speak German though my parents had not yet learned English and spoke in German to me.

¶ During the war my granny spent some time with us but it made me unhappy—I had completely dropped German and couldn't converse with her. I could understand every word but was too stubborn and self-conscious to speak it.

¶ I had forgotten all German by the time I was twelve, and only began to learn it again when I was sixteen. My younger sister has not learned German again at all.

¶ When I found after the war that my mother was alive and I started writing to her, I could hardly remember any German and we just wrote to each other now and again.

¶ During the war I didn't speak German at all, nor did my parents. I took it up for my School Certificate to make things easier for myself and although I hated the language I could not help getting a distinction.

¶ Much against my wish, when I went to university I was persuaded to take a degree in German. I barely scraped through and my parents couldn't understand it 'with all your natural advantages'.

¶ I had to re-learn much of my German when I got a job as translator—my vocabulary was that of a child of eleven.

¶ When I began to take part in broadcasts from Bush House, in the European Service, broadcasting in German, I found that my pronunciation had to be frequently corrected.

¶ My German isn't very good, I have no opportunity to speak it. The only thing I still do is I count in German.

¶ I find it impossible to read any books or see films connected with the European war or with Germans. Although I talk German fluently I do not like using the language unless I have to.

¶ I never went to any other than art-school in this country and have therefore no formal education in English, but I like the language and prefer to read English rather than Czech or German. I find it difficult now to write well in German and feel that I have lost absolute command of any language. My ties with both German and Czech culture are still strong.

¶ Although I was already fourteen when I came I don't express myself well in German and find it very difficult to read and understand. My son and daughter speak German no better than their schoolfriends and like them have learned it as a foreign language at school.

¶ I found myself unable and unwilling to teach my children German as they grew up, although when they began learning it at school I was both willing and interested to help them.

¶ For some time German seemed like a foreign language to me, but since taking up contact with friends and relations on the Continent again, I am just about bi-lingual.

¶ I am married to a fellow refugee and we always speak English at home, but appreciate that we can occasionally (if all other words fail us) express ourselves in German.

III

¶ We always refer to Nazi Germany, but an English person doesn't make that distinction.

¶ I could never bring myself to adopt Nazi doctrines of nationalism and intolerance—I would feel that as a degradation of my whole personality.

¶ While I hate the Nazis, I cannot hate the German people because this would be racial discrimination and would be no different from anti-semitism. In any case, nobody in his right mind can blame German youth for the crimes of their parents.

¶ I can speak and think of Germany and the Germans quite rationally and distinguish between those who actually did all the dirty work and those who actively tried to help the oppressed.

¶ My attitude towards the German people is friendly, many people were only children themselves at that time and we cannot blame them for what happened and many Germans did not enjoy what was going on.

¶ The past is unforgivable but the present generation cannot be burdened with the blame, so one must work towards a reconciliation.

¶ I regard the German people of my generation and older with mistrust and very often hate, but I have nothing whatsoever against the new generation and have had many of these girls in my house as 'au pair' girls throughout the last ten years.

¶ My attitude to the Germans is hostile and will always remain so. I would not, however, teach my children to hate Germans.

¶ Can one legitimately distinguish between the Nazis and the German people as a whole? Well, yes. One has to, not only for historical reasons but also for the sake of one's sanity. I have developed a kind of split mind about Germany—subjectively I wish them all to hell, do unto them what they did unto others.

¶ I always ask myself whether I would have had the courage to hide someone or to defy an official order. I don't feel part of the German Kulturkreis and can therefore reject the Germans without reservation. I don't want to go there or to see them. I love their literature and their music, but I don't want to hear their language spoken. For some irrational reason I don't consider the German spoken by Czechs as real German. I do not want to instil hatred in my daughter, but I think she should know what happened and that it happened where it did. I could not tolerate a German maid in my house because I could not trust myself to treat her justly. It would not be true to say that I don't feel hatred and a wish for revenge, because I think these are the only possible reactions. I think it is unnatural and suspect if people feel differently about this in our situation.

¶ My family, all my relations on both sides, were practically wiped out by the Germans. . . . I use the term advisedly since, so far as I am concerned, Germans and Nazis are virtually synonymous.

¶ I do not hate the Germans for their crimes as I feel too strongly that if I hadn't been a Jew, with my mental make-up I might easily have been a war-criminal myself.

¶ I will never forgive the Germans and what little power I have will always be used against them—i.e. the power to buy goods that are not German, spend holidays in places other than Germany, etc. But this is clearly illogical and the best way to prevent a recurrence of their ghastly deeds is, I am sure, to live in the present and live with them. The Germans I meet nowadays I am really unable to put into the same category as the murderers of Auschwitz.

¶ I would like to think that I have no prejudice for I feel strongly on apartheid and the like. I do sometimes find myself resenting West German affluence and efficiency, and our recent purchase of a Volkswagen took some doing.

¶ My attitude to Germany and the Germans is rather mixed. It varies between cynical admiration of their revival, to deepest revulsion about their past deeds.

¶ I have no hatred of Germans as such; but I believe that one must keep reminding them of what the Nazis did and not support any firm known to have collaborated.

¶ My attitude to Germans is hostile unless I am satisfied by their age, or firm knowledge of their past, that they could not have been active Nazis and are therefore entitled to be excused from the national guilt of their countrymen. I positively boycott German goods and products and will always readily buy a British product which is less perfect or more expensive.

¶ I can't really say I hate them as a people—although I'm not a person who thinks there is anything necessarily wrong with the feeling of hating. I just dislike them very very much.

¶ Germany is a very attractive country, and in fact even my Viennese husband loves holidaying there. And the Germans are just people as far as I am concerned.

¶ As a scientist I must be international. Hence I cannot refrain from associating with Germans and often visit there, both Federal Republic and DDR. Being a professor, I am rather a well-known character over there. It makes me feel a little odd, and many former Germans over here and elsewhere also wonder why I am friendly with German colleagues. But in spite of all that has happened that is how I feel I should proceed. I have similar close ties with Japanese scientists.

¶ There is no future in hating; besides I am not capable of sustained hate. If I advocate conciliation it is not from any Christian (or for that matter, Jewish) spirit of forgiveness, but from a sheer, almost cruel sense of necessity. There is no other way. German resistance to Hitler—and it should not be dismissed as insignificant—I regard as a symbol of redemption, but I do not feel that Germany as of to date has fully redeemed herself. There are still—oh so many—Germans who have learned nothing and forgotten nothing.

¶ I think the Germans, even the new generation, must continue to hate the Jews because they must feel that it is because of the Jews that they have put themselves so much in the wrong with the world. I fear that their children may be misled, but I cannot think them guilty, any more than I am guilty of the death of Christ.

¶ I hope and believe that I could feel at home in any part of the world including Germany, provided I found friends.

IV

¶ As far as reparation is concerned, many of the people I know in the same position as myself obtained reasonable amounts of money from Germany, and although at times we had misgivings about accepting, it was needless to say welcome.

¶ I was very reluctant at first to cash in on something I preferred to regard as a stroke of fate, but finally put in all my claims and now look upon my little fortune as being equivalent to assorted legacies that non-refugees seem to collect from time to time as the older generation dies.

¶ For many years I refused to make any claims. Only after it was put to me that any claims so abandoned will leave money or assets in the hands of those who are most guilty, did I agree to run the usual claims in support of my older brother. I do not depend on the proceeds and treat them rather like a lucky win from the football pools. I have somehow remained emotionally quite unconcerned about the reason for receiving this money.

¶ Whenever I had to fill in detailed descriptions and information, I was resentful. How can anyone pay for the life of a human being? Remembering German officialdom I dreaded the two visits I had to make to the German Embassy. I need not have felt so uneasy for everyone was most polite!

¶ It has taken me twenty years to get back a small part of what I lost and involved endless correspondence which each time upset me afresh. It gave me no satisfaction in the end, as it could not bring back my parents or anything of personal or lasting value. It

5*

only served to re-open wounds over and over again, never letting one forget. Nothing and no one can ever compensate us for the childhood we were deprived of, the friends we were not allowed to have, the education that was denied to us.

¶ The Germans restituted nothing whatsoever to me although our property was very considerable. But as this was in Bohemia and not in Germany proper, nothing was given back to me.

¶ I did not originally apply, as I found the idea distasteful. I was persuaded to do so last summer and was rather amazed to be told that I had no claim as I was stateless.

¶ We never thought of claiming. Probably we should have done.

v

¶ I never wish to return to the country of my birth, feel only shame . . . they say that one must forgive—but to forget is impossible.

¶ I have never been back to Austria, and have no particular desire to go. If anything, rather the reverse, but this is probably reaction to being told by many people (mainly my parents' generation) just how wonderful it all is and how much I would enjoy it.

¶ I could not go to Germany for a holiday; I would wonder what the older generation were doing during the war. Would not go to Austria, either, because of the language. I couldn't pretend I can't speak it—vanity?—and then there is always: 'Where did you learn to speak such excellent German?'

¶ I have not had the opportunity so far to return to my home town. One part of me longs to see the places of my childhood and to introduce my family to the lovely countryside and one or two friends who still correspond with us. At the same time I don't want to go back and be so vividly reminded of things that hurt even to this day.

¶ I would never in my state of mind to date consider returning to Berlin to live, or indeed to visit Germany unless it is unavoidable. In fact I have only once returned for about thirty-six hours strictly on business on behalf of a British exporter. Even then I crossed the Dutch border before booking the second night's hotel.

¶ I quietly gloated over the destruction of German cities and the undoubted hardships which the German people suffered in the immediate aftermath of the war. As late as 1951, when I paid my first visit to Germany since leaving in 1938, I murmured, when actually seeing the mounds of rubble that were once cities: 'Serves them right, serves them right, serves them right'.

¶ I knew that it was no good even to pretend that it was possible for us returning refugees to carry on in 1945 where we had left off in 1939. When I was released from the Army in 1945, therefore, I decided not to return to my former home town, but to settle in Prague. During that time I lived very comfortably, and yet I became increasingly conscious that in fact I was a stranger in my own country. The seven years which my friends, old and new, had spent under Nazi occupation had left their indelible mark. I, on my part, had to concede that the seven years I had spent in exile had likewise left their impression. Many aspects of life in my country appeared to me alien, and many of my thoughts and actions were considered alien by my fellow-countrymen. I knew I was destined to remain a foreigner wherever I lived. I did feel, however, that in the long run I would be able to enjoy a higher standard of living, and be in a position to provide a more generous future for my children, if I made my home in England. And so I came back to the United Kingdom not as a refugee, but as an ordinary immigrant, seeking employment and a home.

¶ Having spent a recent holiday in Germany, I came away thankful that the war had necessitated our emigration—I found the majority of Germans grossly materialistic, unrepentant and loud.

¶ I have found that on the few visits to relatives my emotions have got the better of me. The old fears returned from the moment I set eyes on the man who inspects the passports. I am insecure, reluctant to walk by myself in the street and pretend I am more English than the English. As soon as I am back on English soil, I feel happy and free, at ease, and would like to hug everyone around me.

¶ After my husband's death people would ask me if I would now go back to Germany, and were rather mystified by my vehement denial of any such intention. I still have an aunt and uncle in Germany, whom I visit each year. But I do not enjoy being anywhere which reminds me of my childhood, I do not care for the German people, and feel that I have nothing in common with them. In fact I feel more English there than at home. I find it quite impossible to talk politics with Germans, even my own relations, and a lot of things there upset me, often quite trivial things. I twice visited my home town, once with my husband alone and again a few years ago with the children, and hated it. I shall never go again, not even to visit my father's grave.

¶ Return trips to Germany have been a horror to me. Today, married to an Englishman and under no pressure, I vow that nothing will get me to return to Germany again. This hate, and hate it is, is bound up with a tremendous feeling of guilt, both in taking the atrocities as if they were my own, and inversely, for having got away so lightly. These very complex feelings ruined my adolescence, painfully prolonged into my twenties. . . .

¶ I know they hated us and many still do—the home is destroyed by bombs, a new generation lives in the town, their social and economic culture is alien, the home probably no longer even belongs in any legal sense. There is nothing there for me.

¶ My personal attitude to Germans in general is ambivalent. I have been there many times since the war, and feel ill at ease with them. The Nazi period in general is taboo, not to be discussed; it is something 'they' did, 'we' never knew. . . .

¶ I know quite a few individual German people whom I like very much, but as an anonymous nation I hate and fear it. As I see people in a German street, the thought often crosses my mind and makes me fear: what did you, little man, do to help kill me? And all the 'big' men, how much profit did they make from my suffering? And will it happen again?

¶ I have returned to Germany several times within the past ten years, sometimes en route to other countries on holiday, and twice to my home town to deal with reparations. After all these times I still have the same feelings towards the Germans that I had when I was a child there, and am never able to relax among them, although I have been in many homes when I have visited. I feel that none are sincere and that any, or every one, of them may have been a Nazi or SS man. My hackles rise when I meet them. I can understand the older refugee, who has been unable to make roots here, returning to Germany, but nothing on earth would induce me to spend one day more there than I had to.

¶ My attitude when I go back to Germany is very belligerent. I feel as though I could do something violent, all the time. I still feel that, after all this time. My feeling has never changed. Something which I can never forgive. I only went over there because my cousin is in the British Forces and he happened to be over there and I went to see him. We had very little contact with the German population. I made it a point to be as awkward as possible and spoke as little German as possible to them. I still look at them and think. . . . I was there immediately after the war and you wouldn't believe that all the millions of party members could have disappeared so quickly, because immediately afterwards there wasn't a single person who had ever been a party member or who knew anything about concentration camps.

¶ I have been back to Germany on a few occasions since 1945. In fact I have close friends in Munich, who sometimes stay with me in England. Through them I have met a cross-section of Germans who never became refugees. My impressions are these: There is only a tiny minority of Germans of my generation (or older) who understand or accept what Germany is guilty of. Their values are so far removed from mine that I feel like a traveller on the moon whenever I find myself in Germany. They have come to terms with their past by combining sentimental self-pity (about war-time bombing, the division of Germany, different frontiers, loss of prestige, etc.) with a complacent pride about their economic miracle and a very common amnesia about their crimes. No one wants to have his nose rubbed in the dirt, but I found to my horror that it was not a question of Jews having to forgive the Germans. It was the Germans who could not forgive the Jews. Of course I am not blind to my own prejudices, so on occasions I invited young Germans to spend their holidays with us. The Germans who came to our house reflected their up-bringing—they knew all about Hiroshima, Dresden, and the labour camps in Russia, but had not been *taught* the implications of Auschwitz, or even that Germany wanted and caused the war.

¶ I don't think about their past, I have a mental block there. I hate watching any war film, or discussing politics, if it's anything to do with Germany. If they show old newsreels I get really upset. I can't bear to think about it. I don't want to discuss it or talk about it with anyone. If I go to Germany and meet the people there I want to find out about their way of life, about the business they do—anything—but not what happened.

¶ I went back to my home town last year. It was completely destroyed and rebuilt and seemed to me like a strange place. There was no emotional connection—except that I was somewhat surprised that my parents could have lived in such a small petit-bourgeois place.

¶ The first time I went back to Austria it was not to Vienna where I was born but a holiday resort. It was invaded by Germans and I felt unhappy and uncomfortable. When we did go to Vienna, it was just like visiting a strange city and understanding the language. I felt much more at ease there than I did amongst Germans.

¶ In 1947 we went to Czechoslovakia on a visit and it proved to be a great mistake. I went to see the house where I grew up and saw only strangers everywhere. Our old flat had been partitioned into three smaller ones and I could hardly recognise my own nursery. I did not see a single face I knew. In Prague I found an old chambermaid and a young Czech who had loved my mother dearly and who wept bitterly. I had considered going back but felt it to be impossible after this visit.

¶ When I returned to Germany for the first time I wondered what my reaction would be—whether I would want to settle down there. I certainly felt very sentimental about it, but I soon realised that I did not want to live anywhere but in England.

¶ We were in Vienna for a few days seven years ago and I felt very strange and out of place there; I'm sure I belong here now.

¶ When I visited my home town for the first time a few years ago, I felt a complete stranger. I cannot say that I have any bitter feelings left, except that I tended to wonder with every German I met what part he had played in the Nazi régime. If one can generalise on this subject at all, there is something in the German character which is alien to me.

¶ In 1948 I stayed a fortnight and though I still speak German tolerably well I felt quite foreign. There was nothing in Germany for me, and when I came back I could not settle down. . . .

¶ I have only returned to Germany once, and then to stay with English friends. I found the experience unnerving, and was not prepared for the many reminders of the past. I try to be rational in my attitude to Germany and the Germans, but find this difficult. There are still so many unanswered questions, but I no longer have the feeling of hatred that I once found overwhelming.

¶ Against my will I was induced to go to Germany by my mother when she received her reparation, to enable me to study for a year at an art school there. I don't know what I expected but I had nothing but kindness shown to me the whole time, and can only state my attitude has somewhat softened towards them, particularly as I only mixed with young students who were too young at the time to know.

¶ I have returned to Vienna several times to visit my family. At first the experience was very strange, because I was revisiting scenes of childhood and therefore felt at home. The knowledge of the treachery of neighbours and 'friends' pulled the other way. This dichotomy, I imagine, will never be solved. In the course of my work I spent three months in Berlin where the feeling was stronger still. On the one hand I delighted in the familiarity of many things with my childhood experiences, on the other hand I was oppressed by the knowledge that it was statistically certain that the people with whom I rubbed shoulders every day must contain among them those who had personally killed and tortured my own people. This ambivalence to things German remains. I do not actually believe in the 'two Germanies', one brutal, duelling and anti-semitic, the other cultured, tolerant and democratic. Personally I believe that all these traits are present in all the German people.

¶ My grandparents went back to live in Germany where they had a lot of money; they had been living in very restricted circumstances in England. My parents would never have gone back to live there 'after having been thrown out' and we were brought up to hate and despise the Germans. After the war, however, when my grandparents were resettled in Germany, we went for holidays there, with money from my grandparents. This seemed to me very inconsistent, but since the people we met were very friendly and showed no signs of enmity, the holiday was enjoyable. So there has always been this ambivalent attitude to the Germans—the dislike that I had been taught to have and the friendship I should have liked to have felt for another people with whom we were no longer at war.

¶ This was a terrific experience. I was twenty-six years old and it was seventeen years since I had been in my native land. Again, the first strange feelings between my mother and me (as when my parents came to England). Then, after an hour or two, we were as though we'd never been parted. When I got back from this holiday I felt more keenly what I'd felt all my life in England: that, though I was no longer a Wienerin, and didn't fit into that way of life, I was nevertheless not quite English. In England, people ask: 'Where do you come from?', detecting something not quite English, and in Austria they hear my English accent and do not think me Austrian. So now, after another three visits to Vienna (with all the family and also with my third daughter alone) I am an Anglo-Austrian. I have a cousin who spends his summer holidays with us each year, sometimes bringing some of his friends with him.

¶ Let's face it: I am sometimes homesick. But I don't know if this is for familiar places, or faces, or for my lost youth, or just Weltschmerz. I have been back to Berlin several times (with U.S. Censorship Div. in 1946, and a couple of times since then, the last time in 1958) and have met old neighbours and visited old haunts. It is a very unreal feeling: to be 'home' and yet not to be 'home'.

¶ My reactions were mixed. I was a stranger in a familiar country, speaking my mother tongue brokenly and with an English accent. I didn't want the Austrians to know I had been born in Vienna, possibly because I was still worried about anti-semitism, or more likely because a refugee returning to his place of origin has neither the prestige of an Englishman nor the status of an Austrian citizen: he is almost stateless. This feeling still persists whenever I visit Austria; but not in England, where I feel 99.99 per cent English. In 1954 I travelled alone to Vienna, staying with my uncle. I was of course much more excited than during my earlier visit to Carinthia and became quite agitated as the train neared Vienna and familiar place-names began to appear on the railway stations. Much had changed (Coca-Cola signs everywhere) and much had remained the same (tram routes, for example). I knew our block of flats had been bombed and rebuilt but I went there all the same. I walked to school, went to the park where I used to play, and visited all the places I could remember (which was quite a lot). I felt most odd—elated in a way at returning to my birthplace, feeling glad that I did have roots somewhere, yet finding the smells, the houses, the clothes and customs strange. The people certainly didn't seem as friendly as English people and I couldn't predict their response if I asked them a question, as I usually can at home. Once again I didn't want the Austrians to know I had been one of them, and was always cross when, on showing my beautiful blue British passport, my birth-place was revealed as Vienna. I wanted to have the advantage over them—to be British, to talk English, and yet to eavesdrop some-times and surprise them with my knowledge of German. In shops I usually spoke German, except when I knew I would get better service by speaking English. On subsequent visits my impressions haven't altered radically, except that I have become less emotional about Vienna and more self-assured. I don't think I could ever live there again permanently but I enjoy occasional visits and could probably stay a year, as long as I knew I could always come home. I could never feel completely safe there, though my uncle seems to have settled down again quite well. He usually intro-duces me as his 'English' niece, without explaining our relation-ship or how I come to be English.

¶ I have many times returned to my native Hamburg, and every time this is a cathartic experience for me. Though I know rationally that it isn't possible, I really still feel I belong there. The nostalgia cannot be eradicated, and I no longer try.

¶ My brother enlisted in the Army. He went over there with the Invasion. He was full of hatred for anything German, he went over there determined to kill anybody and everybody, and to my great relief promptly fell in love with a German girl. They have been married since 1949.

¶ On 9th September 1954 I was granted British citizenship and the following week I received my British passport. On 2nd Octo-ber, fifteen years and three months after I left, I was once again on Austrian soil. It was with a mixed feeling of hate and nostalgia that I made my way to the street where I lived. Vienna had been badly hit by war, but the block of flats where we had lived had been left untouched. 'Do you know the family Deutsch?' I asked the caretaker. No—everyone in the block was new. No one at all who had known me or my family. I spent a week in Vienna. I walked along the streets I had known. Everything was strange—yet familiar. The Prater amusement park where I had so often gone as a child was only a skeleton of its former self. The Ring-strasse was full of familiar landmarks. The old Westbahnhof was gone and a new modern building stood in its place. I caught the midnight train to Ostend. I could not sleep, I had a feeling of guilt. I knew I should really hate this place and its people—but hate just would not come. In fact I fell in love with Vienna all over again. This surely was almost immoral. In the summer of 1960 I began my job as a travel courier; my work would take me mostly to Austria. Here and there, I found traces of Nazism. On occasion people still talked about the old days and I made no secret of the fact that I am Jewish and when the subject arose I would let them know what happened to my people. 'We didn't know what was going on. . . .' You liars—you knew only too well. You happy-go-lucky Viennese watched and took part in beating up old men and women. Have you forgotten 10th November 1938? You respectable middle-aged business people in prosperous Austria of today—have you forgotten the foul deeds of yesterday? I should hate you all! I should—but I don't. One day my firm received a very complimentary letter about me: '. . . We admired above all the knowledge of his country and were greatly moved by his love of Austria'.

¶ I went back with mixed feelings—partly because my feelings towards my home town were not at all clearly defined since my last visit there in 1949 to find out the fate of my parents. Frankly I have regretted the visit this year ever since. For some reason I felt suddenly that *there* was my home. I don't wish to sound sentimental or nostalgic—but when I set foot into the old homestead I realised that, perhaps for the first time in twenty-five years, I belonged. Some kind of love-hate relationship—I don't know, all I know is that I feel utterly alien since I came back—like an 'exile' once more. Perhaps the fact that I was made so very welcome by some old friends, whom I had not seen or even contacted for twenty-six years, helped. I seemed to be able to understand people—perhaps it was their way of life—I wish I knew. Perhaps it was the call of the wonderful mountains which I love so dearly. I still distrust the people there . . . it seems to be the actual country itself which has bewitched me. I had a feeling of being on holiday in 1949, but this year it felt like coming home. There, for the first time, for many, many years I was myself. My feelings on the first return to Germany were nil. I don't think I had any. I just can't understand that now. Perhaps my feelings were numbed without my knowing it? I remember I felt like an outsider—who has been there before—but felt no real connection with the place. Yet the moment I set foot in it this time I felt like kissing each stone of the town.

¶ *Home is where some know who you are.* I wrote this line a few weeks before returning briefly, after twenty-five years, to my home town in Germany—Bielefeld, a large industrial town in the Teutoburger Wald. I had left it at the age of fifteen, in December 1938, after the synagogue had been burned and England and a few other countries hurriedly offered asylum to Jewish children. Exactly three years later, on December 13, 1941, my parents were sent to Riga concentration camp; I have been told that my father died there of a stroke and that my mother was sent on and died in Auschwitz.

I did not return for twenty-five years because I had no reason to go back and because I was afraid. I had thought that it would be a terrible experience. I was wrong: it was—this is the exact word for it—my rehabilitation. It was a liberating, healing experience, one that granted me a feeling of peace, such as I had previously known only after giving birth to a child. Perhaps the comparison explains it: I had attempted something difficult and it was all right.

I had heard, after the war, that a few Jews had returned from the Theresianstadt concentration camp; I had heard that much of the town had been destroyed. This information had been thrust on me; I had made no inquiries; I did not want to know what had become of the Jews of Bielefeld or of the town. I had been cast out, I had turned my back. When I returned, I did not *know* anything. I had planned just to walk about, to look at the place as a sightseer, even as a foreigner; I had not intended to speak, really to speak, to anyone.

To the people who live in a town, the changes matter; when one comes back, as I did, what matters most is what one recognises—and I recognised a great deal. I did not mind the changes—what are twenty-five years in the life of a town that has stood for eight centuries? I still felt at home; the first day I was there I walked about the town and felt at home.

My father, who was an architect, once designed a very modern grocer's shop in one of the narrow streets of the old town; the walls were of pale green ceramic tiles and one, in one corner, bore the verse:

Paul Loewenthal
Hat das Haus ersonnen
Wilhelm Harms
Hat den Draht gesponnen

Haetten wir gewusst,
Was es gekus't,
Haetten wir's gelusst.

I thought that first evening that though my father has no grave, no headstone, this was his small memorial. The shop is still there, so is the verse except for the first two lines: my father's name has been scratched out.

Later I met Jews who still live in Bielefeld—about sixty live there where at the beginning of the century lived a thousand. Only after speaking to some of them did I understand that for me it was still 1938: coming back, forty years old and the mother of four children, I had towards the inhabitants of my home town the feelings I had had as a child. I was afraid. No Jewish fifteen-year-old living in Germany today would know what courage I needed, the following morning, to speak to the owner of the shop—the son of the man for whom it had been built.

I had been told that after the war the German people pretended to know nothing concerning any Jew. I had not expected that any-one would remember my father. When the owner of the shop had promised me that he would have my father's name restored, I went to one of the local newspapers to ask its editor to see that the promise was carried through. I did not expect him to be in-terested.

On my third morning in Bielefeld, the paper printed an article about the plaque and mentioned my return. At once many people got in touch with me, to tell me that they remembered my father, or some house he had built, or that they remembered the family, or me. A stone-mason, who as an apprentice had worked for my father, offered to restore the plaque; a former servant gave me a vase which was a present to her from my mother. I met women who had been my childhood friends; I met the couple who had helped my parents to pack the night before they were transported east.

I am aware that these were not representative Germans: they were people who wanted to meet me, a few who remember some Jews with affection. But they were Germans, Bielefelder Ger-mans whose homes I could enter, to whom I could speak as to friends, whom I believed when they said that they were glad that I had come back. With them I was at home: they share my roots, although they are Germans and I am a Jew.

It has taken me twenty-five years to learn to accept what I am: a German Jew. Instinct had told me that I must make this journey by myself, and now I understand why: to my husband and children Bielefeld is abroad, for me it is still home.

¶ Last year I went back to Vienna to face reality. My attitude towards the Austrian people was without any feeling of bitterness, dislike or reproach, which surprised me: and I felt rather like a traitor to the Jewish people. My son was captivated by Vienna and intends to spend six months at the university there before going up to Cambridge. Having hardly any living relations he was looking for my roots and found them in the people of Vienna.

SUMMING UP

I

What makes a Jew is history no less than doctrine.
                                            —*David de Sola Pool*

¶ A refugee is someone fleeing from political, religious or racial persecution, or from the threat of it.

¶ A refugee is someone compelled by reasons beyond his control to flee his home.

¶ A refugee is someone who flees from oppression inflicted on his person or his mind.

¶ A refugee is someone who is obliged to flee for his safety.

¶ A refugee is someone who is forcibly uprooted from his home and therefore has to live in a foreign country.

¶ A refugee is someone who is not wanted in one place and given shelter in another out of pity. He is therefore forced to choose between death and charity.

¶ A refugee is I, you or they if circumstances decree it. It is a survival which is unglamorous, often sordid, and has to be made the best of. It is a state to shake off as quickly as possible.

¶ As long as he wishes to return to his country of origin he remains a refugee even to himself. But once he ceases to feel the urge to return he just becomes an uprooted individual in an at best indifferent alien community.

¶ He ceases to be a refugee when the circumstances which forced him to flee no longer exist, i.e. as soon as he is free to return to his home country. He ceases to be a refugee when he remains in the place where he has found refuge from choice and not out of necessity.

¶ A refugee is a person without a country and as soon as he can grow roots and create a home in a new country and accept this country it becomes a part of his life. I feel that England is my home, although the English will never accept me as one of them-selves. The English differ in this from other nations, and make me very conscious of being foreign. But being foreign is not the same as being a refugee.

¶ I think most of us were ordinary and after a period of adjustment settled down to become just that again or nearly so, bearing in mind Weizmann's dictum that 'Jews are just like other people only more so'.

¶ I am glad of course that I came to England and realise it was the only course open to our parents, though I could not understand this at the age of nine.

¶ I shall always be grateful *now* for what was done for us then, although I wish it had not been rammed down my throat so much as a child who after all does not understand what wars and being refugees are all about. Now I understand better and I could have given my love and gratitude even in those early days if love had been given to me more freely.

¶ Now that I have children of my own, I can appreciate what an ordeal it must have been for my mother to send us away, not knowing where, and whether she would ever see us again—and also I can understand and appreciate how hard it must have been to take a strange child into your home—not to expect anything from it—but to give it the love you give your own. . . .

¶ My story is not outstanding. . . . It is one that was sad for a time, left many unhappy memories imprinted on my mind, which only time can suppress, but unfortunately never erase, and I thank God that I managed to escape from all the horror and found peace, happiness and contentment in this wonderful free country, England. For a long time during my adolescence my sleep was disturbed by piercing nightmares, I used to wake in terror and had a tremendous feeling of insecurity.

¶ My early experiences in England were very unfortunate. I had no one to confide in, no one who tried or even wanted to understand. There was that awful feeling of helplessness about my parents and all my fears about them. Since those experiences I have never been able to feel really deeply about anything.

¶ One felt for a long time that everything was only temporary, a sustaining thought which never entirely left me until a letter from a friend of the family after the war confirmed what really I had known for a long time and had not admitted, that my parents were dead and it was all a permanent violent disruption the effects of which were to last a lifetime.

¶ It took me a long time to emerge from a sort of mental block that I had been under regarding the earlier part of my life, and to realise more fully the true enormity of what had happened to me and a whole generation of people. I began to realise my impotence to alter it all. . . .

¶ Memories of my family and odd episodes connected with my past sometimes come to my mind quite unexpectedly. It was only as I grew older that the full horror of the atrocities which had been committed became more and more vivid in my mind. How can one possibly describe the bitterness and regret one feels for the deliberate and terrible destruction of so many innocent human lives?

¶ When I got married and my husband and I both became British citizens, the severity of the fate of our families began to register properly. One began to try and make a normal life for oneself and to learn, not to forget but to live with these thoughts.

¶ My childhood becomes more important to me as I grow older, the knowledge of my parents' fate becomes a greater burden, because when I was younger I did not think about it.

¶ You cannot ever really be happy again when your parents have been killed in concentration camps.

¶ I have wondered whether our parents did the right thing to send us here—we were only one quarter Jewish and they survived the war in Vienna. Yes! Of course they did. They wanted the best for us, and England was hospitable. Has my life been worth saving? I hope and believe so. One thing it has done: here is a European-minded family. Neither all English nor Austrian—a little cosmopolitan. And I hope the wiser and kinder and more sympathetic for the extra understanding which this gives us.

II

¶ Home is the first place one knows. One can be happier later on, one can live in a house much superior to the one in which one grew up. But home is the place in which one is neither privileged nor resented; one just belongs there.

¶ Home is where you were a child.

¶ Home is the place where you have been brought up and have lived for as long as you can remember.

¶ I don't know how to define home. I remember what it felt like to wake up in the nursery during the winter months or to come home from school through the snow. Maybe one only feels at home in the first place of one's emerging consciousness—where one first became aware of one's surroundings.

¶ Home is where your nearest and dearest are—if you've got any. If you haven't there is no home.

¶ Mixing with other people most of whom do have a home of their own, the meaning of home is likely to become more and more exaggerated.

¶ My home is a house not a home. What I remember is a dream of home.

¶ Home is the place where you 'belong'. I still think of 'home' when I think of my childhood, but it is no definite place.

¶ I think it is usually assumed that if you came young enough to have a completely English education and to learn to speak English without an accent you cannot have found it impossible to become settled and altogether English. But those of us who were youngest usually came with our parents and our parents were still refugees when we grew old enough to understand. We never had the settled background of other children; our parents weren't able to inspire us with much confidence in themselves. It might even have been better to be without them, from the point of view of not being torn between two worlds, of being able to stop being a refugee and becoming entirely English.

¶ Originally, when we came, it was for two years and nothing was ever decided or said during the war to make me think that I would even be able to spend the rest of my life in England. I did not begin to think of settling down here until after I knew that both my parents were dead and that I did not even have close relations anywhere else. And then I was already over twenty. So, *in my mind*, I did not come as a permanent settler until I was adult.

¶ I did not want to cease being what I believed myself to be—and that included my Vienna background.

¶ My life changed completely when I became a refugee. The direct results for me were the loss of the parental home, lack of a satisfying career, an early marriage with consequent loss of religious contact and lastly material shortcomings in the early days of my independence and marriage. For my children it has meant lack of contact with their grandparents and other relations, which had so enriched my own childhood.

¶ Being a refugee has meant to me a hatred for the Germans who were responsible for killing most of my family and therefore spoiling my life, and my difficulty in forgetting the past and settling down to a new and happy life. I feel England is a good country to live in in different circumstances, but because of my difficulties I may perhaps consider leaving this country in the hope that somewhere else I might forget the past and start a new life. But I doubt whether life would be different for me in another country.

¶ I know now that I can never be free of the past, it is with me forever. My father committed suicide the year I got my degree, he could never accept the difference in our lives. Being a refugee has meant and means that I don't belong anywhere. I lead a very full life, I run a home for four children and teach full time in an infant school, I am active in local amateur dramatic groups. I am never free from insecurity and I am always afraid, this is of course something that does not show, even my husband is unaware of the depth of panic that can still overwhelm me. My father is dead; his nine brothers and sisters were deported and died. My grandfather died in Theresienstadt. I live a very normal and successful life, but I am always oppressed by the past, I don't know any people like me, and therefore find it difficult to make lasting contacts. Being a refugee means or has meant for me that nowhere is home, and that I can never really fit in anywhere.

¶ My career has gone remarkably smoothly, I am very happily married, and seem, to almost everyone who knows me, an exceptionally fortunate person. Nevertheless, I have never known what it is to feel really at home. When I go back to Germany I smell blood (many members of my family were killed by the Nazis, and my father, who managed to escape, died before his time because he could not live with the consciousness of what had happened to his nearest relatives). And in England I feel, in spite of all, that my family and I are living on an island of our own. I feel Jewish, yet cannot take an interest in Jewish affairs (or more than a purely intellectual, theoretical interest in the Jewish religion). My constant melancholy may be congenital, but is it not improved by my feeling of rootlessness.

¶ I don't think I'd be any better off in any other country. Feel I don't really belong anywhere.

¶ It has left me with a permanent feeling of inadequacy intellectually and even emotionally, and perhaps a feeling of always being at a slight disadvantage.

¶ One thing which stands out now and is probably due to my earlier life is that I loathe uncertainty, that is I like to feel above all secure, although I am an impetuous person.

¶ Although reasonably successful in my career, I am often socially ill at ease, despite the fact that I enjoy gregariousness. I am not able to form easy friendships, and have few personal friends.

¶ Over the years, life for me has not changed very much, I am still single and not happy in my way of life, which is, I think, mainly due to my difficulty in getting on with people. I feel that all this has been brought on by the fact that I came to England at an early age and was separated from and later lost my family. This is, of course, not the fault of England, to which country I am very grateful for opening its doors to me at the critical time. Otherwise I would certainly not be alive today. I like England and I feel that it is a good country to live in.

¶ I still live like a refugee in a bed-sitter in Hampstead. This is partly because I lack any sense of permanency.

¶ I do not feel at home in England but doubt whether one can feel at home anywhere except in the surroundings of one's early youth. I do not mind feeling rootless for myself, but fear that my daughter, who has only me in this country, will suffer in this respect. She lives comparatively isolated now. . . . Perhaps an all out conscious effort to acclimatise would have helped but I never found any English people who felt that we belonged here and the fact that we only have to open our mouths to establish ourselves as outsiders is sufficient in itself.

¶ I still retain a thick accent. Only the other day a greengrocer, thinking me a recent arrival, congratulated me on my progress in idiomatic English. I remain, on the whole, a foreigner.

¶ Most of my friends and acquaintances are also people from the Continent, who came over the same way as I.

¶ When meeting other refugees one does not feel an outsider.

¶ If we had not remembered that we were refugees there were always others to remind us.

¶ I have had phases of wanting to be integrated, trying to be integrated, and assuming I had integrated. Now I realise that a fellow refugee, who claimed that we could never integrate owing to a radically different background, was quite right. I think the reason is that the social classes are differently constructed here, and the type of person I am and the interests I have (built up from heredity and early environment) just can't find the exact social strata. I don't think this has so much to do with a different language and/or geographical background—which it might in the case of, say, an Eskimo—it is just this different sense of values.

¶ I feel that I am a mixture, partly still refugee. I can go about my business without me or others being conscious of it. But just a single word, just a slight incident and I can become extremely aware of it. I imagine I will now stay like this. It hardly makes me different from someone English-born. Just a certain sense of identity.

¶ By outward appearance, manner, accent, no one ever suspects that I'm not English. Yet I feel inside that I have at least as many characteristics from a Jewish, refugee background as from an English one.

¶ Despite being integrated and recognised (I am a member of the local Council) there is the odd occasion when one is given to understand that not having been born and bred in this country means being a foreigner, even in a cosmopolitan community.

¶ Now, with my wife and a few friends and my work, I have settled down to a life that is remote from those early struggles and misfortunes and my outlook of life is of England and this culture, but always there is an awareness of apartness. Although one expects that as time goes by these things will matter less, I think a part of one will always be—a refugee.

¶ Although I might in practice identify myself completely with my present way of life, I would never be regarded as an Englishman.

¶ Although I am married to an Englishwoman and have two very English daughters, I have never cherished any illusions about becoming fully assimilated into an English background. I regard myself as a German half-Jew, and have never tried to pretend to be anything else. I have travelled quite a bit, and when all is said and done I regard the English people as the kindest on earth, but I know I can never be one of them. I am, and always shall be, a foreigner.

¶ Owing to our experience in Germany, I do not think that we will integrate any further than we have done up to the present merely because we cannot believe that we can ever integrate completely into the community. This feeling does not seem to be reflected in our children, who look on our experiences only as interesting and exciting.

¶ It seems like yesterday that everything happened. I have been back to my home town, and I have cried many tears for the family and friends I loved and who are no more. I pray that my daughter will never know such horror, that she will be able to hold her head high and not cringe with fear at the word 'Jew'. She is being brought up as a Jew, with a heritage to be proud of, and I shall tell her everything when she is old enough to understand. As for me, I try not to hate but it is difficult. I cannot look at a German without wondering if perhaps he was one who did unspeakable things to people—nor do I ever want to go to Germany again. Perhaps it is better to forget the past, if one can. Most of the time I feel completely integrated, I feel, think and dream in English. It is when I am together with English Jews that I still feel different—our outlook on life in most cases is worlds apart.

¶ A friend and I recently agreed that since adulthood not only did we find that we were used to a different culture from English Christian people but that sometimes we felt nearer to them than to the bulk of the Anglo-Jewish community. On the other hand we felt ourselves equally far removed, we agreed, from the German Jewish community.

¶ Religion holds little place in my life and it is many years since I went to synagogue; owing to what happened to my family I can no longer believe. But I could never cease to be a Jew, or to be proud of being one.

¶ After the war I began to lose my faith, though I was at the same time an ardent Zionist. Up to then I had said my prayers regularly in bed, praying for my parents' safety. When I found out that my prayers had been ignored and that six million Jews had perished, I just couldn't believe in God any more.

¶ As far as religion goes, I have none, despite a basically C. of E. education, and an adolescent urge to be baptised. This I recognised as merely a wish to attach myself to a big organisation which has endured through the centuries. Basically I am pro-religion, anti-Church. I am conscious of my Jewish heritage in a vague way—I attended synagogue recently for the first time for years . . . very interesting, I was an outsider yet not an outsider. I am certainly conscious of being Jewish at times. My husband wanted our son to be circumcised for hygienic reasons. . . . I said NO—this would mark him as a Jew, and you never know. . . . I suppose I am still afraid.

¶ My marriage with a Catholic was a fight against my religious roots and I find myself suffering more under it than I would have believed. I love my children and grieve deeply that they are being educated in another religion.

¶ My children to a small extent suffer what I did in childhood. In school they are asked why they call my mother *Omi*, they do not go to church, they know Mummy was born in Berlin. I hope they can accept the difference more than I could.

¶ Our children are missing the valuable relationships of grandparents, as both of us are orphaned; and as we both happen to be only children as well, ours have no aunts, uncles or cousins. We speak English at home, so they have no opportunity to become bilingual naturally, but we never disguise the fact that we were born and brought up in another country, and had another language originally.

¶ Both of us feel that our children need to be aware of the fact that they are Jewish. My husband would like to bring them up as humanists but this seems too difficult for a child; besides, I'm not sure I don't believe in God. This quandary now brings back the feeling of being refugees. We feel we have more in common with some of our non-Jewish friends. This area is English-Jewish; we contemplated sending the children to the local Reform Synagogue for classes since their friends go there, but the difference in their home background would then be underlined. Why need they be Jewish? Not to bear the burden of our experience. Partly because it is a matter of pride, mainly that is what they happen to be and I do not want them to deny it. This perplexity is not exclusive to refugees but intensified by not belonging.

¶ We're ethnically Jewish, but not religious. We *feel* that we are Jewish, and in some ways different from other people. At the same time, we are rather militant atheists. This is going to be very difficult to put over to the children. We shall have to try and do it. We owe that much to the Jews who were murdered. They, the children, won't be able to 'pass' just because that's easier.

¶ I think one of the worst consequences was that I had a great hatred of my parents for a long time, especially of my mother. I should have been old enough to understand why she sent me away but because she tried to be reassuring about their own safety I just did not know—and when I found out that they had both died in concentration camps I thought for a long time that they must have deserved it. I think now this was because I just could not admit to myself what a terrible loss they were to me, and so I pretended that I was well rid of them. One persisting effect of all this is that I have no idea what they were really like and there is no one to tell me.

¶ My sister and I became separated during the war—she has become acclimatised in Italy and I have become acclimatised in England. So that when we meet we are so different now, we might almost be coming from different families, entirely different backgrounds. And when we talk about our mother and father they might be two different sets of parents—because we were at different stages of adolescence when we left home we remember them quite differently. Incidentally, because of the different languages we can barely talk to each other's children.

¶ For a long time I did not concern myself with being a refugee. I assumed that this was something I would grow out of. When I first realised that returning to my home town was something I was capable of doing, I thought that the experience would liberate me from the past, in the sense that afterwards the past would no longer matter to me. Instead, I have been liberated only from the fear of the past, which means that there is now nothing between me and it: it matters to me as if it had all happened recently. This is the most difficult thing I have ever had to face: that my Jewish childhood in Nazi Germany and my orphan exile at the age of fifteen must remain a part of my life always: it will never be as if it had not happened, I shall never be 'just like anybody else' (which was the bait with which my parents lured me away). Since I am the sum of my experiences, to try to ignore my past would be a kind of insincerity. I am not the same as I would have been if I had not been uprooted; to think about this is not morbid but constructive: an attempt to learn something about human nature. I am not the same as the people amongst whom I live; this does not mean that I am inferior, but simply different. Not to recognise this difference is also a kind of racialism: to believe that Jews and Gentiles are really the same implies the assumption that if they were not they would not be equals. I believe in Adler's theory of compensation, which has been illustrated by the Jews throughout the centuries: a handicap is really a sort of advantage. I am what I am not in spite of being a refugee but because of it. The terrible past is not an adversary but my greatest asset: I will not fight against it but put it to work. I cannot alter what has happened but by making a tool of it I can at least give it a purpose.

¶ And if, twenty-five years ago, I was still willing to be labelled a German, I am not now. This is the respect in which I am uprooted for life.

¶ I am still a refugee because my roots are where I am not.

¶ I am still a refugee because I have never found contentment or peace.

¶ I am still a refugee because the scars inside me are too deep, and on so many occasions each year they are opened afresh.

¶ I am still a refugee because I still feel different. I can't seem to feel at home here or anywhere else. I react differently to situations, my whole attitude to life is different from that of the people around me.

¶ I am still a refugee because I had to flee from the country of my birth and this has profoundly altered the shape of my whole life and will influence it until the end of my days.

III

¶ Home is where you have been living and consider you belong. But if all your family went away, I don't think it would be home any more.

¶ Germany was never 'home' but only a memory—I left at the age of three with my parents and retain fleeting memories of earliest childhood concerning it.

¶ Home is where you can relax and live a normal life, making your own decisions, living at peace with neighbours, and free to live as you wish.

¶ Home is where one feels one belongs and where people are nice to one.

¶ Home is where one can live with a feeling of permanency.

¶ Home is with my children.

¶ Home is where one feels settled, together with one's family, where one finds one's livelihood and where one feels one belongs to some sort of community, however small.

¶   Home is where one chooses to live and is welcome to stay.

¶   Home is the place where our family or friends are and in that sense it is not confined to one country or part of the world.

¶   I don't think it makes any difference now that I was a refugee. Just as anyone might have a hard time, I had a hard time—I wouldn't have had it otherwise but I feel proud of having overcome it.

¶   On looking back I feel that those very strange and hard years were probably a very good education for me and contributed a good deal towards forming my attitude to life.

¶   I feel in no way deprived, and I believe that I have been able to make the most of what ability I am endowed with. The particular problems of being a refugee have had a stimulating effect and have probably given me more drive than I would otherwise have shown. The one sad aspect of my immigration was watching my mother working as caretaker, cook, housekeeper, etc., during the war in order to eke out an existence for my father and herself. She did this with tremendous cheerfulness and it was my goal from the age of fourteen to ease her lot.

¶   My parents and my earlier life began to fade from consciousness and seemed almost to belong to someone else's existence, an impression which has become stronger year by year ever since.

¶   Being separated from my mother all through the war was obviously no joke, though the wrench was far worse for her, as children are so adaptable. My sister and I soon settled down to our new life in England. We have grown to love this country and would not dream of returning to Germany. I suppose we felt like refugees at the beginning, but for so many years now this has seemed our natural home, that one never remembers the feeling of being a refugee with all its connotations. Of course I remember Berlin, and speak German, but after twenty-five years here the first ten years seem remote. . . .

¶   I have never found anybody unfriendly because of my German origin. I have always been able to adjust myself to changing circumstances and make friends. I feel completely at home in this country and have done so for a very long time. I feel no bitterness towards the Germans but I do feel that I have been cheated out of some important things, education mainly. I would not like to go

6

back to Germany to live but would like to visit there. To me it now seems like a foreign country. In other ways I have no doubt gained insight into other people and am happy to be able to speak three languages. All the same I hope that our children will not have to run away and move about as I did. There are better ways of learning languages.

¶ Being a refugee has not been a problem for me. I was six when I left Germany, too young for 'my country' to mean anything to me, and because I grew up in an English and a Christian family, I have identified completely with my adoptive country. I am not obviously Jewish so that it was easy for me to become accepted as an English girl; but living with two mothers has been a great problem.

¶ Having been a refugee no longer bothers me in any way, though I remember that during the war years I was very conscious of the fact that I was from Germany.

¶ It was, after the war, when I first became independent, that I ceased to feel like a refugee although most of my friends were refugees. I was no longer homesick and had come to appreciate the British way of living and the character of the people in this country. And I was determined that this should be my home.

¶ I found it relatively easy to become assimilated. This seems to show that most of the barriers between one man and another are purely man-developed, and anything that sets out to maintain them, whether it is a religion, or a feeling of class, or of race, is undesirable (to put it mildly).

¶ I see nothing in what has happened to feel that I have something to be ashamed of. If people ask me why I have a foreign-sounding name, I tell them the reason: that I was a Jewish refugee from Germany.

¶ I certainly don't feel outcast, on the contrary by being open about my origin and Jewishness, background and past I encounter invariably respect and sympathy and no real detriment socially or in business.

¶ When people ask me I say I came from Germany before the war—I don't mind being asked. I don't particularly explain that I am Jewish—before the war is such a long time ago that it doesn't matter now.

¶ I have now been in England for well over two-thirds of my life. To admit to my German nationality no longer causes me any embarrassment; rather, it makes me smile—because it seems to me as if I were talking of another person. I am no more German than a Chinaman who happens to be born while his mother's junk passes through German waters. Any official form that comes my way today I fill in as follows: Religion—none. Nationality—English. It may not be factually quite accurate but psychologically it is 100 per cent true.

¶ Today I am a happy wife, mother and business woman, and I seldom remember my un-English origins. Occasionally, if I meet someone with an obviously European background, I may ask where they come from and we chat about our histories, but that is all, it is history for me now. And yet, it has made me what I am, and what I am proud to be . . . very individualistic, very idealistic.

¶ I can speak German but not very well (although with no accent); we always speak English at home and it is my language of choice. I think I have become more English than anything else, although there are Viennese traces in our life—food, entertaining, reading, music, *Gemütlichkeit* etc.; and, of course, we lead a definitely Jewish life: much more so than I had with my parents.

¶ Socially I am completely integrated into the English background. We have close friends who are English Jews and non-Jews, and Jews of Continental origin, and mix equally well with all.

¶ The men who work under me have accepted me, never questioning my original background, perhaps in fact being more friendly because of it. My wife and I do not find it difficult to make social contact, through our church activities we meet a large variety of people, which we both enjoy. . . . I feel that my position and aim must now be to try and help create as good an understanding between my country of birth and this country. I owe much to both countries, never forgetting that we are all children of God.

¶ Our new parents were deeply patriotic, and this feeling they succeeded in communicating to me. Today, I am far more aware than most people of the deep traditions of England, and am very proud to be British and that our children will be English (that oh-so-subtle distinction). I do feel gratitude for the policy which let us children in, so much so that while technologists are needed here, emigration seems almost traitorous, although opportunities abroad are more numerous and attractive than here. I like to travel but always feel happy to get back to England, dear safe old England.

¶ It was probably as an undergraduate at Cambridge that I was able to see the experience of being a refugee for the first time without tension and in perspective. I now felt that there was some advantage in having access to two cultures and could now appreciate some aspects of German culture with more sympathy and less bitterness, while integration was no longer a problem or something to be striven for. I do not wish to minimise the problems involved in being a refugee. A lot of energy has to be expended, at any rate for a time, on matters which most people can take for granted. With a small daughter, I am just beginning to notice that there is one thing I have really missed: English child culture, Beatrix Potter *et al.* . . . . May be I shall catch up on this now.

¶ This is not a fairy tale and so I shall not end with 'happily ever after', for life is a little complex and I could write some sour notes about the difficulties of foreigners, albeit naturalised, who are but self-educated, i.e. semi-educated, in obtaining jobs with prospects. Nevertheless, I managed to struggle through. I cannot boast any outstanding achievements, but here I am in early middle-age in the middle ranks of management with a middling sort of income. Away from the mundane I would like to state, with a small voice, that I am happily married, we live in a pleasantly situated flat which we call home and I have long ceased to regard myself as a refugee. I am happy to live in this country and would even make bold to say I love it, warts an' all.

¶ This feeling of belonging and being able to join a group of people on equal terms I think meant to me a tremendous lot and still does. I think to me this was the most important issue of all: to be accepted in a community on equal terms.

¶ I am a strong and active member of the Labour Party, ward secretary, local election candidate, etc. Not once has anyone in the Party commented on the fact that I am not British born. This for me symbolises the greatness of this country.

¶ I believe the outstanding impact the British made on me at first and still do sometimes today is their consistent resistence to officialdom ruling the people and the individual. Coming from

Germany where the uniform, the policeman, the official, were supreme, I have never really ceased to be amazed and thrilled at the frequent acceptance by authorities here that they are our 'obedient servants' and the intermittent stand that persons make against the strongest rules, persons of rank, and government.

¶ I am certainly grateful for the influence the English way of life has had on me. I value the English people's readiness to let others be themselves and their respect for a different way of life however much it opposes their own, and not least of all the easy friendship which is happily extended without making any demands in return.

¶ I don't think my children ever think of me as German. They know that my father and mother are German, they always call them *Oma* and *Opa*, and their father's parents are grandma and grandpa. They must be aware that they are different from other children. But nowadays that is exciting. When I was young it wasn't, and you just kept quiet about it.

¶ As I feel no personal bitterness towards the Germans and the fact of my being a refugee plays no part in our present lives, I think my children just regard it as a natural circumstance. Sometimes it is even an advantage: different, interesting people they meet. Now that they are bigger the fact that I speak French and German is a help to them at school.

¶ Although my children do not feel any different from their friends, certain difficulties do arise. For example, we eat in the continental way, so that there are careful enquiries as to what we are having before bringing home a friend to supper. That is another thing, we do not have high tea but supper about seven, an inconvenient time often, as all English people have finished their meal by then. Also we celebrate Christmas Eve and give presents then, which intrigues their English friends. Since my girls are older I have told them of their Jewish blood (I am a Catholic) and they find it rather interesting, but of course they do not have our attitude. They were very puzzled when I asked them not to tell this to all their friends, and I found it quite impossible to explain my feelings to them. As to language, they understand German very well, but speak and write it badly, and are learning it at school from scratch. We never speak German at home.

¶ I am no longer a refugee because, although it implies being different, it implies homelessness much more. We do not fit in completely because we are Jewish yet not Jewish enough for English Jews. I am no longer a refugee because my husband and I are lucky enough to have a home; our relatives are scattered all over the world but they have all settled somewhere; the fact that we have children who are English makes me feel that we are not refugees any more and in the security of that feeling I can teach them that they belong to a much larger unit than simply a nation or a race or a particular religion. To have been a refugee helps one to keep a sense of perspective in regard to apartheid, for instance, and one can explain principles to one's children in the light of that experience.

¶ We have two boys; they are being brought up with a pride in their religion and race, in addition to regarding themselves as British. They are aware that their parents are not British born, and seem to have accepted this peculiarity without undue questioning or getting any complexes. They are happily normal.

¶ I am aware that I am Jewish and the rest of the family have this awareness, but as an atheist I do not have much contact with organised religion.

¶ Although my husband and I and our children are Jewish and have never thought of being anything else, we are completely non-practising.

¶ Our children, like ourselves, are agnostic. They, however, have had 'scripture' taught to them as one of the ordinary school subjects. We find that this has made no difference to their agnostic outlook; on the contrary, they are in a better position to qualify their agnostic belief simply because they know the Bible.

¶ My children have not been christened. They will have to make up their own minds which, if any, religion they wish to follow. The fact that I am Jewish intrigues them somewhat, they are apt to forget it but I remind them; on the whole it does not crop up very often.

¶ My children were not baptised until they were in their early teens, at their own request. I talked it over with them and my son was also confirmed. Actually I think that he was so keen on it because his best friends were being confirmed at the same time and he hates to be an outsider. I don't think my decision was connected with the fate of my parents, not consciously, anyway.

¶ My eldest son was baptised when he was twelve. I didn't want to influence him in any way. I thought if they are baptised they are bound to be Protestant or think they are Protestant; I wanted them to be of an age when they could decide for themselves. He had not reached that age but he was a choir boy and he loved it and I thought that anyway it's already gone to one side. . . . It might do more harm than not if he isn't baptised—in a Christian country. The important thing is that he should feel that he belongs.

¶ I have four children and hope to have more. One needs relations. My children when they grow up will need relations. It could so easily come about that they would be lonely if there were only two or three—one might die and another might emigrate. There is nothing I can do about the past generation but I can insure myself against being left alone in the future.

¶ I am not aware of being a refugee, only of being an exile.

¶ On the surface I no longer consider myself a refugee, but know quite well that it takes only a small reminder to bring back the refugee feeling.

¶ I don't feel a refugee any longer but I feel that I am without roots.

¶ I am no longer a refugee because I no longer feel the need of physical and moral help. I do have problems, both physical and spiritual, but I feel more ready to grapple with them than I once did, and am no longer as willing to relapse into self-pity, to blame external circumstances and long for outside help to extract me from my difficulties. To me one of the greatest dangers and tragedies of being a refugee is that one loses one's identity, one's self-respect and the ability to cope with new situations.

¶ I am no longer a refugee because I lead the same sort of life that I would lead if I had been born here. That I don't *feel* perfectly integrated doesn't really matter—it might just be my peculiarity or an over-awareness of basically small differences.

¶ I am no longer a refugee because I don't feel different from an ordinary English person in enough ways. And I don't feel hard done by—which is perhaps one of the salient defining characteristics. It is a fact that my background is different from that of people here, and therefore it must be a fact that I *am* different in some ways. But I feel that I'm just one of the heterogenous elements in the community.

¶ I am no longer a refugee because I have made my way in the society to which I came as a refugee. I no longer, if ever, feel that my country of birth is my home. I am British though I shall never be English.

¶ I am no longer a refugee because I have a permanent home in a place of which I have absorbed the culture and traditions and whose language is my natural means of expression.

¶ I am no longer a refugee because I have put down roots (of sorts) and have practically forgotten my country of origin.

¶ I am no longer a refugee because my home is now here. My 'German' characteristics have not entirely disappeared (how could they?) but are adaptable to my status as a new Englishman.

¶ I am no longer a refugee because I became one at an age when a child's desire to be like his fellows is very strong. After a short time I spoke without an accent. I have no particular racial characteristics in appearance so it is easy to be one of a crowd. My early marriage has perhaps contributed most to my integration.

¶ I am no longer a refugee because I love my adopted country, and although I lived abroad much during the last fifteen years it was amongst English people. I like the way of life, and think it is a good country in which to bring up my children.

¶ I am no longer a refugee because I have severed all connection with the country of my childhood, and have lived nearly twice as long in England as originally in Germany.

¶ I am no longer a refugee because I have severed all links with the past, and have started a completely new life.

¶ I am no longer a refugee since I married and have my own home, friends and family.

SIX POEMS

THE CHILDREN'S EXODUS

I

It was an ordinary train
travelling across Germany
which gathered and took us away
those who saw it may have thought
that it was for a holiday
not being exiled being taught
to hate what we had loved in vain
brought us lasting injury

II

Our parents let us go
knowing that who stayed must die
but kept the truth from us although
they gave us to reality
did they consider what it meant
to become orphaned and not know
to be emotionally freed
when our childhood seeds were spent

III

When we went out of Germany
carrying six million lives
that was Jewish history
but each child was one refugee
we unlike the Egyptian slaves
were exiled individually
and each in desolation has
created his own wilderness

IV

This race-hatred was personal
we were condemned for what we were
no one escaped the ritual
from which we rose inferior
the blood-guilt entered every home
till daily life was a pogrom
we who were there are not the same
as those who have no wreck to share

V

Home is where some know who you are
the rescue was impersonal
it was no one's concern what use
we made of the years given us
one should not ask of children who
find their survival natural
gratitude for being where
ten thousand others have come too

VI

At Dovercourt the winter sea
was like God's mercy vast and wild
a fever to a land-locked child
it seemed fire and cloud to me
the world's blood and my blood were cold
the exiled Jew in me was old
and thoughts of death appalled me less
than knowledge of my loneliness

VII

My mother sold my bed and chair
while I expected to return
yet she had kept me close to her
till I saw our temple burn
it was not for her sake but mine

she knew that I was unripe fruit
and that exile was a blight
against which one prepared in vain

VIII

People at Dovercourt were gay
as if they thought we could forget
our homes in alien play
as if we were not German Jews
but mealtimes were a market-place
when sudden visitors could choose
although we were not orphaned yet
a son or daughter by their face

IX

My childhood smoulders in the name
of the town which was my home
all we were became no more
than answers on each questionnaire
at Dovercourt we were taught that
our share of the Jewish fate
had not been left behind but was
the refugee life facing us

CAST OUT

Sometimes I think it would have been
easier for me to die
together with my parents than
to have been surrendered by
them to survive alone

Sometimes it does not seem that they
spared me the hardest Jewish fate
since by sending me away
they burdened me and cast me out
and none suggested I should stay

When the Jews were branded there
was one number meant for me
that another had to bear
my perennial agony
is the brunt of my despair

Sometimes I feel I am a ghost
adrift without identity
what as a child I valued most
for ever has escaped from me
I have been cast out and am lost

THE TOWN

I did not want to feel at home
of what importance was the town
my family were driven from
how could I still have thought it mine
I have four children why should I
expend my love on stones and trees
of what significance were these
to have such power over me

As stones and trees absorb the weather
so these had stored my childhood days
and from a million surfaces
gave back my father and my mother
my presence there was dialogue
how could I have refused to answer
when my own crippled childhood broke
from streets and hillsides like a dancer

TO MY CHILDREN

Others may pity me but you shall not be ashamed
how can I scorn the life which is all I have
I will not belittle the little that I have saved
by denying my childhood memories my love

How can I wish to undo the past which I am
though I beggared myself I would not become another
'the appalling Jewish experience' is my own
'the unknown victims' are my father and mother

Be proud of the beginning you have in me
be proud of how far I have wandered with this burden
I would value you less if I were not a refugee
your presence changes my wilderness to a garden

I WAS NOT THERE

I

The morning they set out from home
I was not there to comfort them
the dawn was innocent with snow
in mockery – it is not true
the dawn was neutral was immune
their shadows threaded it too soon
they were relieved that it had come
I was not there to comfort them

II

One told me that my father spent
a day in prison long ago
he did not tell me that he went
what difference does it make now
when he set out when he came home
I was not there to comfort him
and now I have no means to know
of what I was kept ignorant

III

Both my parents died in camps
I was not there to comfort them
I was not there they were alone
my mind refuses to conceive
the life the death they must have known
I must atone because I live
I could not have saved them from death
the ground is neutral underneath

IV

Every child must leave its home
time gathers life impartially
I could have spared them nothing since
I was too young – it is not true
they might have lived to succour me
and none shall say in my defence
had I been there to comfort them
it would have made no difference

RACE

I

When I returned to my home town
believing that no one would care
who I was or what I thought
it was as if the people caught
an echo of me everywhere
they knew my story by my face
and I who am always alone
became a symbol of my race

II

Like every living Jew I have
in imagination seen
the gas-chamber the mass-grave
the unknown body which was mine
and found in every German face
behind the mask the mark of Cain
I will not make their thoughts my own
by hating people for their race